# MAURICE RAVEL

# Valses nobles et sentimentales

for Piano Solo

Edited by / Édition de / Herausgegeben von
Roger Nichols

Urtext

# EDITION PETERS
LONDON · FRANKFURT/M. · LEIPZIG · NEW YORK

Peters Edition Limited
Hinrichsen House
10–12 Baches Street
London
N1 6DN
England

Tel: +44 (0)20 7553 4000
Fax: +44 (0)20 7490 4921
e-mail: sales@editionpeters.com
Internet: www.editionpeters.com

© Copyright 2008 by Hinrichsen Edition, Peters Edition Limited, London

All rights reserved. No part of this publication may be reproduced, stored in a retrieval system or transmitted in any form or by any means, electronic, mechanical, photocopying, recording or otherwise, without the prior written permission of the publisher.

Music setting by Jon Holmes, The Note Factory

Printed in the UK by Halstan & Co. Ltd, Amersham, Bucks.

# CONTENTS

Preface .................................................................... iv
Préface .................................................................. viii
Vorwort ................................................................ xii

## Valses nobles et sentimentales

I ............................................................................. 1
II ............................................................................ 4
III ........................................................................... 7
IV ......................................................................... 10
V ........................................................................... 12
VI ......................................................................... 13
VII ........................................................................ 16
VIII ...................................................................... 22

Critical Commentary ........................................... 26

# RAVEL'S PIANO MUSIC – A NEW EDITION
## Editorial Method and Sources

There is no denying the excitement of holding in one's hand the autograph manuscript of a musical masterpiece; and where the autograph is itself a work of art, as many of Ravel's are, then aesthetic considerations also come into play to compound the excitement. But there is equally no denying that composers are, like all mortals, fallible, and that however beautiful and exciting an autograph is, it may nonetheless contain mistakes. The apparently laudable desire to go back to what the composer originally wrote needs therefore to be tempered with a certain amount of common sense.

With stage works, it is true, pressures of time, space, money and personalities often lead to deformations which the composer does not in any sense welcome but has to accept if the performance is to go ahead, and which may then find their way into the printed score. But in the case of piano works, the pressures on the composer in preparing an edition are much slighter, exerted for the most part by the printer in his desire for conformity with house style, so that changes introduced between manuscript and edition have a somewhat greater chance of representing decisions freely taken by the composer. Certainly, in the process of publication mistakes may be introduced as well as rectified and, when musicality and common sense indicate that this may have happened, the autograph can indeed sometimes provide vital evidence. But in the course of conversations with a number of composers of our own time, I am given overwhelmingly to understand that they would actually be angry if future editors ignored their carefully prepared printed scores and went back automatically to their original autographs for a so-called true reading.

In the case of Ravel's piano music, such a critical view of autograph evidence is more than ever justified, since the Music Department of the Bibliothèque nationale de France holds a bound volume containing Ravel's own printed copies, with autograph corrections, of the bulk of the first editions of his solo piano music.[1] To judge from the contents, the volume would appear to have been made up between 1911 and 1913. The works missing from this collection are *Sérénade grotesque*, *Sites auriculaires*, *Ma mère l'oye*, *Prélude*, *A la manière de...*, *Le tombeau de Couperin* and *Frontispice*. Printed copies with autograph corrections of *Ma mère l'oye* and *A la manière de...* are held separately in the same institution,[2] while Ravel's own printed copy of *Le tombeau de Couperin*, with autograph fingerings and one autograph correction, is on display in the Musée Ravel at Montfort l'Amaury. For *Sérénade grotesque* and *Sites auriculaires* the autographs may be said to assume paramount importance since these pieces were not published in the composer's lifetime. The autograph of *Frontispice* is also significant because Ravel's own printed copy has not been found. Unfortunately, for *Prélude* neither the autograph nor the composer's printed copy is extant.

No proofs are known to survive of the first editions of any of Ravel's piano works, apart from a set of first proofs of *Le tombeau de Couperin* in the Durand archives, marked up by the Durand editor with a request for second proofs (I am grateful to Roy Howat for providing me with a copy of this material). This set contains no autograph markings. All the editorial annotations found their way into the first edition except for the form of some of the multiple appoggiaturas in 'Prélude' and 'Forlane' of *Le tombeau de Couperin*, over which Ravel would seem to have changed his mind.

### Primary Sources

Where Ravel's own corrected edition is available, I have taken it as my main primary source; discrepancies between this corrected edition (**CE**), the first printed edition (**E**) and the autograph are duly noted.

The autograph of *Valses nobles* (nine pages in the Taverne collection) has not itself been made available for study, but a microfilm (**AM**) is held in the Music Department of the Bibliothèque nationale de France (Vm. micr. 876).

### Secondary Sources

The secondary sources fall into four groups:

(a) Printed copies with corrections by musicians close to Ravel

(i) Copies of Ravel's piano music belonging to Robert Casadesus (**CasCE**), now also housed in the Music Department of the BnF; his copy of *Valses nobles* is shelved as Vm. Casadesus 940. It contains no markings in the composer's hand.

(ii) Some copies, including that of *Valses nobles*, belonging to Vlado Perlemuter (**PerCE**), also now housed in the BnF, but awaiting cataloguing.

(iii) Some copies with corrections by Lucien Garban. Garban worked for the Durand publishing house and was a close friend of the composer. The exact status of these corrections is impossible to determine but, given the links between the two men, it is feasible that at least some of the changes were dictated by Ravel. These copies are now in the library of Bakersfield College, California. Garban also made piano duet transcriptions of *Valses nobles et sentimentales* and *Le tombeau de Couperin*. These are published by Durand.

(iv) Copies not consulted include those belonging to Jacques Février, whose niece and pupil Mme Aboulker-Rosenfeld has assured me that they contain no markings beyond his fingerings; and those of Henriette Faure, which cannot be located.

(b) Ravel's own orchestrations of a number of his piano pieces (**RO**). In chronological order of original composition (dates of orchestration in brackets), these are: *Menuet antique* (1929), 'Habanera' from *Sites auriculaires* (1908), *Pavane pour une Infante défunte* (1910), 'Une barque sur l'océan' and 'Alborada del gracioso' from *Miroirs* (1906 and 1923), *Ma mère l'oye* (1911), *Valses nobles et sentimentales* (1912), 'Prélude', 'Forlane', 'Menuet' and 'Rigaudon' from *Le tombeau de Couperin* (1919).

(c) Recordings

(i) Piano rolls made by Ravel in 1913 for Welte-Mignon (*Sonatine*, movements I and II, C2887; *Valses nobles et sentimentales*, C2888), and in 1922 for Duo-Art (*Pavane pour une Infante défunte*, 084; 'Oiseaux tristes' from *Miroirs*, 082). It was claimed that at this second session Ravel also recorded 'Le gibet' from *Gaspard de la nuit* and the 'Toccata' from *Le tombeau de Couperin*, but these were in fact recorded by Robert Casadesus. It remains uncertain which of the two recorded 'La vallée des cloches' from *Miroirs* in 1929 for Duo-Art (72750), though I am almost certain it was Ravel. All these recordings have been transferred a number of times to LP, but unfortunately the piano roll equipment has not always been properly regulated.

(ii) Recordings made on disc by three pianists, all of whom had the benefit of the composer's detailed advice: Robert Casadesus (1955, CBS 13062–4[3]); Jacques Février (1972, ADES 7041–4); Vlado Perlemuter (1961, VOX VBX 410 1–3[4]; 1977, NIMBUS 2101–3, reissued CD NI 5005, 5011). Marcelle Meyer, although known to Ravel (together they gave the private two-piano performance of *La valse* which failed to impress Diaghilev), never studied his piano music with him, as her daughter, Marie Bertin, was good enough to inform me. I have therefore taken no account of Mme Meyer's Ravel recordings reissued by EMI on the Référence label.

(d) Souvenirs of Ravel as a coach of his piano music

(i) from Vlado Perlemuter in his interviews with Hélène Jourdan-

Morhange, published as *Ravel d'après Ravel* (Lausanne, 1953) and in an English translation by F. Tanner as *Ravel according to Ravel* (New York/London, 1988; 2/1991).[5]

(ii) from Vlado Perlemuter in conversation with the editor of the present edition.

(iii) from Henriette Faure in *Mon maître Maurice Ravel* (Paris, 1978) (**FauS**). Mlle Faure, the sister of the politician Edgar Faure, was coached by Ravel for her recital of his music – in all probability the first ever all-Ravel piano recital – which she gave at the Théâtre des Champs-Elysées on 12 January 1923 (not 18 January, as she states in her book), when she was eighteen. Her daughter, Mme Mayette Constantin, kindly informed me that at one time she had in her possession her mother's original notes, taken directly from Ravel's instruction, but that these were lent to a researcher and never returned. Other souvenirs are fully identified *in situ*.

The secondary sources are considered when they shed further light on an established text, or when problems in the text are not fully elucidated by the primary sources.

## Acknowledgements

I should like to express my gratitude to the following for their assistance: to Gaby Casadesus for information about her husband Robert; to Dr Michel Noiray, who told me about the autograph of *Sonatine* and helped me to obtain a copy; to James Segesta, reference librarian of California State College, Bakersfield, for sending me copies of Lucien Garban's corrected scores; to Jean Touzelet, and later to Denis Hall and Rex Lawson, for allowing me to hear Ravel's Duo-Art piano rolls on machines in perfect order; and to Dr J. Rigbie Turner, Curator of Music Manuscripts and Books in the Pierpont Morgan Library, New York, for sending me copies of the autographs of *Jeux d'eau*, and of 'Noctuelles' and 'Oiseaux tristes' from *Miroirs*. I am grateful also to various performers; to Vlado Perlemuter for talking to me about his lessons with Ravel and for allowing me to study his copies of the music; to Roy Howat for advice that has blended the scholarly with the practical; to Junko Okazaki for providing me with a photocopy of Perlemuter's copy of the *Valses nobles*; and to Michael Channon, Anthony Goldstone and Charles Timbrell for their views about the tam-tam in 'Laideronnette' and other details in *Ma mère l'oye*. Finally, my thanks go to the staff of the Music Department of the Bibliothèque nationale, and to Margaret Cobb, Graham Hayter, Olivier Mazal, Gwendolyn Mok, Jean-Michel Nectoux, Dr Arbie Orenstein, and Dr Stephen Roe for numerous kindnesses.

[1] Originally Vma. 2967, now reshelved as Rés. Vma. 493

[2] Vma. 3157(7) and Fol. Vm12. 2701(2)A respectively

[3] Reissued SONY MH2K 63316

[4] Reissued VOX CDX2 5507

[5] Dual page numbers refer to the French and English editions respectively

# VALSES NOBLES ET SENTIMENTALES
## Preface

The first performance of *Gaspard de la nuit*, given by Ricardo Viñes at the Salle Erard in Paris on 9 January 1909, established Ravel once and for all as a major composer, and dispelled any lingering doubts that he might merely be a Debussy clone. But the appearance of his next keyboard work, *Ma mère l'oye*, on 20 April 1910 at the inaugural concert of the Société musicale indépendante (SMI), did little immediately to further his reputation – indeed, actually caused disappointment to some who had seen Ravel as the coming man. There was therefore no doubt keen interest to hear what his following major keyboard work, *Valses nobles et sentimentales*, would bring.

The SMI, which Ravel had played a large part in founding, was dedicated to opposing what he regarded as stuffiness and pomposity in French musical life, and specifically in the concerts of the Société nationale, where Vincent d'Indy's influence had come to predominate. Just as putting *Ma mère* into the first concert had been a blow for freedom, so was the policy at the society's 13th concert on 9 May 1911 of playing all the pieces anonymously, with the nine composers' names revealed only at the end – and after the audience had had a chance to guess them. The *Valses* were played by Louis Aubert, a minor composer whose greater claim to fame is perhaps that as a boy he sang the 'Pie Jesu' in the first performance of Fauré's *Requiem*. Quite a few guessed Ravel correctly, but there were also votes for Satie and Kodály, among others. More awkward for Ravel was to have to sit through hoots and protests,[1] and to hear close friends afterwards condemning the *Valses* as unmusical and even cacophonous.[2] It is worth noting that, although the SMI continued to exist until 1935, this experiment was never repeated.

To a large extent, the audience can be cleared of blame. In his autobiographical sketch Ravel refers to 'a style that is simpler and clearer, in which the harmony is harder and the lines of the music are made to show up.'[3] He refers also to the example of Schubert, whose collections of *Valses sentimentales* (D779, 1823) and *Valses nobles* (D969, 1827) together supplied Ravel's title – an influence that seems to have gone little further than that, although Roy Howat has pointed out that in the opening of the first Valse Ravel borrowed the rhythm of Schubert's first *Valse noble*, but shifted it one crotchet later so that Schubert's upbeat now becomes a downbeat.[4]

As with *Jeux d'eau*, Ravel prefaces the score with a quotation from Henri de Régnier, but whereas there the quote evokes the mood of the piece, the heading to *Valses nobles* appears to be anti-evocative: 'le plaisir délicieux et toujours nouveau d'une occupation inutile' ('the delightful and ever novel pleasure of employing oneself without a purpose'). Dancing is essentially 'inutile' and, like this piece, its own justification. The parallel may be taken further. The tension between the formal steps of a dance and the emotions of the dancers on the floor is mirrored in the tension between the tightly controlled phrase structures and their expressive content, which is not always what we expect. Indeed the violinist Hélène Jourdan-Morhange, in conversation with Vlado Perlemuter,[5] drew attention to the unusually large number of 'expressif' and 'très expressif' indications in the score – 14 in all, five of them in the Epilogue.

However, the quotation is arguably more objective when one reads the Régnier novel from which it is taken. *Les rencontres de M. de Bréot*, published in 1904, is the tale of an *éducation sentimentale*, at the end of which the young M. de Bréot looks back over his adventures, just as the final Valse of Ravel's work recalls previous ones:

> ". . . .when M. de Bréot thought of the various things that had happened during his stay in Paris, a city famous for offering all sorts of experiences, he could not help concluding that, for his part, he had observed no more than ordinary events and none of the sort that turn you into another man. M. de Bréot was still M. de Bréot, for himself as for everyone else. He thought the same thoughts as before and committed the same actions. It is true, even so, that his thoughts also dwelt on the memory of various fairly unusual characters who, when it came to it, had made it worth his while to leave the provinces, thanks to the interest ('curiosité') of their acquaintance and the pleasure ('agrément') of their company."[6]

A combination of 'curiosité' and 'agrément' is a tempting description of Ravel's musical style in general and of the *Valses nobles* in particular, where these qualities are joined by the rhythmic constraints of the dance. Harmonically, the style is, as Ravel says, of a new hardness after the shimmering sumptuousness of pieces such as 'Ondine'. This comes about not so much through 'new' chords as through the plainer presentation of old ones, and until the epilogue, where the 'various fairly unusual characters' of the earlier waltzes are reviewed through the haze of memory, the piano's atmospheric capabilities are largely shunned. The tension referred to above is partly achieved in the first Valse through the interweaving of chromatic scales with the bass 'circle of fifths' progressing through all 12 notes of the scale, and Ravel arranges that the return of the initial D (in bar 61) coincides with the return of the opening material.

Writers have frequently mentioned the bitonal texture in the central section of the seventh waltz, which Ravel thought the most characteristic of the *Valses*.[7] At this stage of Ravel's career the bitonality is always resolved and does not attain the contrapuntal independence we find in the *Duo* or in *L'Enfant et les sortilèges*. An excellent example of this kind of resolution, achieved through persistence, is to be found in the last 35 bars of the Epilogue, where the bass G asserts itself over all comers and has the last word – a marvellous fusion of technique and poetry. In the novel, M. de Bréot and Mme De Brionne likewise achieve union in the final pages.

The *Valses* have never been the most popular of Ravel's piano works, and he was even heard to refer to them as 'maudites' (cursed).[8] By 1987 they had sold some 70,000 copies as against 120,000 of *Le tombeau de Couperin* or 250,000 of the *Sonatine*. However, 40,000 of those 70,000 had been sold since 1971, suggesting that pianists were, finally, beginning to catch up with Ravel, albeit 60 years later.[9] The truth is that the *Valses* are very hard to play well, posing formidable problems of pedalling, of manual independence and, strangest of all, of *rubato*, normally anathema to Ravel. Where phrases in 3/2 and 3/4 times are presented simultaneously (in bars 7–10 of the first Valse, for example) Ravel insisted that both rhythms must be heard. Perlemuter recalls that Ravel made him repeat those four bars ten times, hands separately, and remarks on the composer's attitude to the work: 'I remember with a certain emotion the sight of Ravel, sitting at his desk near the piano, score in hand, while he took me through these *Valses*. I had never seen his eyes so bright – he was so determined on being understood, on letting nothing slip by either in the notes or, just as much, in their interpretation. Through this passion for perfection in the letter, one found oneself automatically in tune with the spirit.'[10]

Henriette Faure's experience was similar: 'he got up, stood near the piano and put me through a torture that half a century has not allowed me to forget, stopping me continually, picking me up on the smallest details, for a breath, a silence, a pedalling, an inflexion . . . and behind all that, like a clock at the end of a corridor, his inexorable 1 2 3 1 2 3. . . . It was exhausting, one had to integrate fantasy with rigour and produce dreaminess or elegance within an extreme of rhythm and precision. This martyrdom lasted nearly two and a half hours.'[11]

Some of Perlemuter's and Faure's more general comments on the individual Valses are worth recording here (their comments on particular bars or phrases are noted in the Critical Commentary):

I  'There must be strength and sonority, but not hardness.' (**PerS** 43/44) This waltz 'alternates percussive passages with waves of expressive legato.' (**FauS** 39)

II  Of the dynamic 'hairpins' in this Valse, 'Ravel never found them emphasised enough.' (**PerS** 44/46)

III  'The difficulty in this third Valse is to isolate the third beat; this produces a hesitation before playing the first beat [of the following bar].' (**PerS** 44/46) 'The third Valse is a tiny, precise, chiselled mechanism, with alternations of passages that call for a short, sharp movement of the wrist and steely fingers within a pianissimo, with phrases of expressive, undulating legato. Here too the rhythm must be strict, allowing very fleetingly for a few gentle, expressive rallentandos, but which Ravel wanted to be very short and to be returned immediately to control.' (**FauS** 39)

IV  'As usual, Ravel wanted the hairpins emphasised, but without slowing down.' (**PerS** 46/48)

V  Perlemuter's score is headed with the manuscript inscription: 'Dans l'esprit d'une Valse de Schubert'. But it is not, as he claims, in Ravel's hand, though almost certainly was dictated by him. The same applies to other annotations, similarly claimed in **PerS** as being by Ravel. 'When we were working on it, Ravel suggested the title "Venetian Waltz" to help get across the Romantic Style. Ravel wanted this Valse to be like a doll made of silk and velvet; he suggested to me the title "Valse 1830".' (**FauS** 40–1)

VI  Here again, Perlemuter stressed the importance of bringing out the binary rhythms in the left hand: 'It's the only way to weld this passage together and bring it off as Ravel demanded.' (**PerS** 50/52)

VII  For details, see Critical Commentary

VIII – Epilogue   'Ravel was so passionate about the unity of tempo here that I must be insistent about it. It is also one of the interpretative difficulties in this Valse . . . Ravel wanted the epilogue to be slow, but for it to keep its waltz rhythm.' (**PerS** 53–4/56–7)

Over a mere fortnight in March 1912 Ravel orchestrated the *Valses* to form the ballet *Adélaïde ou le langage des fleurs*. The impresario responsible for the venture was Jacques Rouché, who had just directed the ballet version of *Ma mère l'oye* at his Théâtre des Arts at the end of January. Ravel's ballet formed a quadruple bill at the Châtelet theatre on 22 April with Dukas's *La Péri* (also being premiered), Schmitt's *La Tragédie de Salomé* and d'Indy's *Istar*. Each composer conducted his own work and the occasion was billed as a *Concert de danse*, N. Trouhanowa – the ballerina who figured in each work. The concert premiere of the orchestral version was given on 15 February 1914, conducted by Pierre Monteux.[12]

It is widely felt that this orchestral transcription is one of Ravel's most astonishing achievements. The temptation for an editor therefore must be to take back into the piano solo score all the markings from the orchestral one. But an autograph message among Ravel's effects[13] carries the general caveat: 'nuances accents points liaisons peuvent et doivent souvent être différents dans la transposition d'orchestre' ('nuances, accents, dots, slurs can and often must be different in the transcription for orchestra'). The key word here is 'often'. Despite Ravel's warning, there are some places where the orchestral score (**RO**) does offer undoubted help over interpretation, and these instances are duly referenced in the Critical Commentary. At all events it would be a hardhearted teacher who would actively discourage pupils from listening to Ravel's magical orchestrations.

## Editorial Practice

All editorial additions are marked in square brackets. Round brackets indicate either readings taken from secondary sources, in which case details are supplied in the Critical Commentary, or cautionary accidentals from **AM** and **E**; there is also a single editorial cautionary accidental in bar 58 of the Epilogue. Fingerings are Ravel's, taken either from **AM** or from **CE**, as noted in the Critical Commentary.

Pedal markings in **AM**, reproduced in **E**, are sparse: two in Valse II, and a number of *3 cordes* and *sourdine* markings in the Epilogue. There might be a case for taking pedal indications from **RR**. But, against that, not only was Ravel a mediocre pianist (as his performance of Valse I in particular testifies), but his 1913 recording was his first encounter with the medium and, as is generally acknowledged, in stressful situations pedalling is one of the first things to suffer. The markings in **GarCP** coincide only partially with those observed in **RR**. Since there are no additional pedal indications in **CE**, where Ravel had every opportunity of inserting them, it seems best in general to leave pedalling to the player's discretion. Exceptions are made in those places where Perlemuter or Faure have particular instructions to pass on, or where the pedalling in **RR** is both interesting and likely to be unaffected by Ravel's technical deficiencies: in these instances, the information is conveyed in the Critical Commentary.

### Table of Source Abbreviations

**AM**: autograph on microfilm

**E**: first edition, published by Durand, deposited at the BnF on 28 December 1911 (D&F. 8247)

**CE**: Ravel's corrected copy of the first edition

**CasCE**: printed copy with Casadesus's additions and corrections

**GarCP**: printed proof copy with Garban's additions and corrections

**GarT**: Garban's piano duet transcription, published by Durand in 1918 (D&F. 9549)

**PerCE**: Perlemuter's printed copy with Ravel's additions and corrections

**RO**: Ravel's orchestral transcription, published by Durand in 1912 (D&F. 8476)

**RR**: Ravel's recording on piano roll

**CasR**: recording by Casadesus

**FévR**: recording by Février

**PerRI** and **PerRII**: recordings by Perlemuter (the designation **PerR** without a number indicates that Perlemuter's two recordings coincide over the point in question)

**PerS**: souvenirs from Perlemuter in *Ravel d'après Ravel*, in conversation with Hélène Jourdan-Morhange

**FauS**: souvenirs from Faure in *Mon maître Maurice Ravel*

*Roger Nichols*
*2007*

[1] 'Esquisse autobiographique', *La Revue Musicale*, (Dec 1938), 21

[2] Louis Aubert to Manuel Rosenthal, who related it in conversation to the editor

[3] see note 1, *ibid.*

[4] R. Howat, *The Piano music of Debussy, Ravel, Fauré and Chabrier: explorations and illuminations*, Yale, 2008, ch 17 (I am grateful to the author for allowing me to see this book in typescript)

[5] **PerS** 44/46

[6] *Les rencontres de M. de Bréot*, Paris, Mercure de France, 1904, 272–3

[7] see note 1, *ibid.*

[8] Roland-Manuel, quoted in **FauS** 37

[9] I am grateful to Maison Durand for allowing me access to these figures

[10] **PerS** 42/43

[11] **FauS** 20

[12] for further information, see Deborah Mawer, *The Ballets of Maurice Ravel*, Aldershot, Ashgate, 2006, 125–148

[13] contained on a microfilm in the BnF, Vm. micr. 860

# LA MUSIQUE POUR PIANO DE RAVEL – UNE NOUVELLE ÉDITION
## Principes d'édition et sources

Nul ne niera combien il est émouvant de tenir en main le manuscrit autographe d'un chef-d'œuvre musical ; et lorsque l'autographe est lui-même une œuvre d'art, comme c'est souvent le cas de ceux de Ravel, cette émotion est encore renforcée par les considérations esthétiques. Mais nul ne niera non plus que les compositeurs sont, comme tous les mortels, faillibles, et qu'un autographe, si beau et si émouvant soit-il, peut néanmoins comporter des erreurs. Le désir louable de retourner à ce que le compositeur a écrit à l'origine demande donc à être tempéré par un certain bon sens.

Avec les œuvres scéniques, il est vrai que les questions de temps, de lieu, d'argent et de personnes conduisent souvent à des déformations dont le compositeur ne se réjouit nullement, mais qu'il doit accepter pour que la représentation aille de l'avant, et qui peuvent se trouver incorporées à la partition imprimée. Mais, dans le cas d'œuvres pour piano, les pressions sur le compositeur dans la préparation d'une édition sont bien moindres, exercées pour l'essentiel par l'éditeur, qui souhaite qu'elle se conforme aux usages de la maison, si bien que les changements introduits entre le manuscrit et l'édition ont une plus grande chance de représenter des décisions librement prises par le compositeur. Certes, dans le processus de publication, des erreurs peuvent aussi bien être introduites que rectifiées, et lorsque la musicalité et le bon sens indiquent que c'est le cas, l'autographe peut effectivement apporter un témoignage crucial. Mais des conversations avec un certain nombre de compositeurs de notre temps m'ont convaincu qu'ils seraient en fait très agacés si les futurs éditeurs ignoraient leurs partitions soigneusement préparées et retourneraient automatiquement à leurs autographes originaux pour une lecture prétendument véridique.

Dans le cas de la musique pour piano de Ravel, une telle vision critique des documents autographes est plus que jamais justifiée, puisque le département de la musique de la Bibliothèque nationale de France possède un volume contenant les exemplaires imprimés de Ravel lui-même, avec des corrections autographes, de la plupart des premières éditions de sa musique pour piano seul [1]. À en juger d'après le contenu, le volume semble avoir été réuni entre 1911 et 1913. Les œuvres qui manquent dans cette collection sont : *Sérénade grotesque*, *Sites auriculaires*, *Ma mère l'Oye*, *Prélude*, *À la manière de...*, *Le Tombeau de Couperin* et *Frontispice*. La même bibliothèque conserve séparément des exemplaires imprimés avec corrections autographes de *Ma mère l'Oye* et d'*À la manière de...* [2], tandis que l'exemplaire imprimé personnel de Ravel du *Tombeau de Couperin*, avec doigtés autographes et une correction autographe, est exposé au musée Ravel de Monfort-l'Amaury. Pour la *Sérénade grotesque* et les *Sites auriculaires*, les autographes sont d'une importance capitale, puisque ces œuvres ne furent pas publiées du vivant du compositeur. L'autographe de *Frontispice* est également important, puisque l'on n'a pas retrouvé l'exemplaire imprimé de Ravel. Malheureusement, pour le *Prélude*, ni l'autographe ni l'exemplaire imprimé du compositeur ne nous sont parvenus.

À notre connaissance, il ne subsiste d'épreuves de la première édition d'aucune œuvre pour piano de Ravel, mis à part une série de premières épreuves du *Tombeau de Couperin* dans les archives Durand, marquées par l'éditeur de Durand d'une demande de secondes épreuves (je remercie Roy Howat de m'avoir fourni une copie de ces documents). Ces épreuves ne comportent pas d'indications autographes. Toutes les annotations éditoriales ont été intégrées à la première édition sauf la forme de certaines des appoggiatures multiples dans le « Prélude » et la « Forlane » du *Tombeau de Couperin*, au sujet desquelles Ravel semblerait avoir changé d'avis.

### Sources primaires

Lorsque l'édition corrigée de Ravel est disponible, je l'ai prise comme source primaire principale ; les divergences entre cette édition corrigée (**CE**), la première édition imprimée (**E**) et l'autographe sont dûment notées.

L'autographe des *Valses nobles* (neuf pages dans la collection Taverne) n'est pas disponible pour étude, mais un microfilm (**AM**) est conservé au département de la musique de la Bibliothèque nationale de France (Vm. micr. 876).

### Sources secondaires

Les sources secondaires se divisent en quatre groupes :

(a) Exemplaires imprimés avec corrections de musiciens proches de Ravel :

(i) Exemplaires de la musique de piano de Ravel ayant appartenu à Robert Casadesus (**CasCE**), maintenant conservés au département de la musique de la BnF ; son exemplaire des *Valses nobles* est coté Vm. Casadesus 940. Il ne comporte pas d'indications de la main du compositeur.

(ii) Quelques exemplaires, dont celui des *Valses nobles*, ayant appartenu à Vlado Perlemuter (**PerCE**), maintenant également conservés à la BnF, mais en attente de catalogage.

(iii) Quelques exemplaires imprimés avec corrections de Lucien Garban. Garban, qui travaillait pour la maison d'édition Durand, était un ami intime du compositeur. Le statut exact de ces corrections est impossible à déterminer, mais, étant donné les liens entre les deux hommes, il est possible qu'au moins certains des changements aient été dictés par Ravel. Ces exemplaires sont maintenant à la bibliothèque de Bakersfield College, Californie. Garban fit également des transcriptions pour piano à quatre mains des *Valses nobles et sentimentales* et du *Tombeau de Couperin*. Elles sont publiées par Durand.

(iv) Parmi les exemplaires qui n'ont pas été consultés figurent ceux de Jacques Février, dont la nièce et élève, Mme Aboulker-Rosenfeld, m'a assuré qu'ils ne comportaient pas d'autres indications que ses doigtés ; et ceux d'Henriette Faure, qui n'ont pu être retrouvés.

(b) Les orchestrations faites par Ravel lui-même d'un certain nombre de ses œuvres pour piano (**RO**). Par ordre chronologique des compositions originales (dates d'orchestration entre parenthèses), ce sont : *Menuet antique* (1929), « Habanera » des *Sites auriculaires* (1908), *Pavane pour une infante défunte* (1910), « Une barque sur l'océan » et « Alborada del gracioso » de *Miroirs* (1906 et 1923), *Ma mère l'Oye* (1911), *Valses nobles et sentimentales* (1912), « Prélude », « Forlane », « Menuet » et « Rigaudon » du *Tombeau de Couperin* (1919).

(c) Enregistrements

(i) Rouleaux de piano faits par Ravel en 1913 pour Welte-Mignon (*Sonatine*, mouvements I et II, C2887 ; *Valses nobles et sentimentales*, C2888) et en 1922 pour Duo-Art (*Pavane pour une infante défunte*, 084 ; « Oiseaux tristes » de *Miroirs*, 082). On a dit que lors de cette seconde séance Ravel enregistra également « Le Gibet » de *Gaspard de la nuit* et la « Toccata » du *Tombeau de Couperin*, mais ces pièces furent en fait enregistrées par Robert Casadesus. On ne sait pas avec certitude lequel des deux enregistra « La Vallée des cloches » de *Miroirs* en 1929 pour Duo-Art (72750), encore que je sois presque sûr que c'est Ravel. Tous ces enregistrements ont été transférés un certain nombre de fois sur microsillon, mais malheureusement à partir de pianos mécaniques qui n'étaient pas toujours bien réglés.

(ii) Enregistrements faits sur disque par trois pianistes qui bénéficièrent tous de conseils détaillés du compositeur : Robert Casadesus (1955, CBS 13062-4 [3]) ; Jacques Février (1972, ADES 7041-4) ; Vlado Perlemuter (1961, VOX VBX 410 1-3 [4] ; 1977, NIMBUS 2101-3, réédition en CD NI 5005, 5011). Marcelle Meyer, qui connaissait Ravel (ils donnèrent ensemble l'exécution à deux pianos de *La Valse* qui ne réussit pas à impressionner Diaghilev), n'étudia jamais sa musique pour piano avec lui, comme sa fille, Marie Bertin, a bien voulu me le confirmer. Je n'ai donc pas tenu compte des enregistrements Ravel de Marcelle Meyer réédités chez EMI dans la collection Référence. Mais je me suis bien entendu référé à l'enregistrement de *Ma mère l'Oye* signé par Casadesus avec son épouse Gaby (1951, Sony Classical MH2K 63316) (CasrgR).

(d) Souvenirs de conseils donnés par Ravel sur l'interprétation de sa musique pour piano et rapportés par :

(i) Vlado Perlemuter dans ses entretiens avec Hélène Jourdan-Morhange, publiés sous le titre *Ravel d'après Ravel* (Lausanne, 1953) ;

(ii) Vlado Perlemuter dans des entretiens avec moi-même ;

(iii) Henriette Faure dans *Mon maître Maurice Ravel* (Paris, 1978) (**FauS**). Ravel fit travailler Henriette Faure, sœur de l'homme politique Edgar Faure, pour le récital – très probablement le tout premier récital de piano entièrement consacré à Ravel – qu'elle donna au théâtre des Champs-Élysées le 12 janvier 1923 (et non le 18 janvier, comme elle le dit dans son livre), à l'âge de dix-huit ans. Sa fille, Mme Mayette Constantin, m'a aimablement informé qu'à une époque elle avait en sa possession les notes originales de sa mère, directement tirées de l'enseignement de Ravel, mais qu'elle les prêta à un chercheur qui ne les lui rendit jamais. Les références d'autres souvenirs sont données dans le texte.

Les sources secondaires sont prises en compte lorsqu'elles jettent une lumière nouvelle sur un texte établi, ou lorsque des problèmes de texte ne sont pas pleinement élucidés par les sources primaires.

## Remerciements

J'aimerais remercier les personnes suivantes pour leur aide : Gaby Casadesus, pour les renseignements sur son mari Robert ; Michel Noiray, qui m'a parlé de l'autographe de la *Sonatine* et m'a aidé à en obtenir une copie ; James Segesta, bibliothécaire de California State College, Bakersfield, qui m'a envoyé des copies des partitions corrigées de Lucien Garban ; Jean Touzelet, et ensuite Denis Hall et Rex Lawson, qui m'ont permis d'entendre les rouleaux de piano Duo-Art de Ravel sur des machines en parfait état ; et J. Rigbie Turner, conservateur des manuscrits et livres musicaux de la Pierpont Morgan Library, New York, qui m'a fait parvenir des copies des autographes de *Jeux d'eau*, et de « Noctuelles » et « Oiseaux tristes » de *Miroirs*. Ma reconnaissance va également à divers interprètes : à Vlado Perlemuter, qui m'a parlé de ses leçons avec Ravel et m'a permis d'étudier ses partitions ; à Roy Howat, qui m'a donné des conseils à la fois musicologiques et pratiques ; à Junko Okazaki, qui m'a fourni une photocopie de l'exemplaire des *Valses nobles* de Perlemuter ; et à Michael Channon, Anthony Goldstone et Charles Timbrell, pour leurs idées sur le tam-tam dans « Laideronnette » et d'autres détails dans *Ma mère l'Oye*. Enfin, ma gratitude va au personnel du département de la musique de la Bibliothèque nationale de France, ainsi qu'à Margaret Cobb, Graham Hayter, Olivier Mazal, Gwendolyn Mok, Jean-Michel Nectoux, Arbie Orenstein et Stephen Roe pour leurs nombreuses gentillesses.

---

[1] À l'origine Vma. 2967, maintenant recoté Rés. Vma. 493.

[2] Vma. 3157(7) et Fol. Vm12. 2701(2)A respectivement.

[3] Réédition SONY MH2K 63316.

[4] Réédition VOX CDX2 5507

# VALSES NOBLES ET SENTIMENTALES
## Préface

La création de *Gaspard de la nuit*, donnée par Ricardo Viñes à la Salle Érard à Paris le 9 janvier 1909, imposa une fois pour toutes Ravel comme un compositeur majeur, et, si certains pensaient encore qu'il pourrait n'être qu'un simple clone de Debussy, dissipa tout doute à ce sujet. Mais l'apparition de son œuvre pour piano suivante, *Ma mère l'Oye*, le 20 avril 1910, lors du concert inaugural de la Société musicale indépendante (SMI), ne contribua guère dans l'immédiat à consolider sa réputation – elle provoqua même une certaine déception chez ceux qui voyaient en Ravel le compositeur de l'avenir. Son œuvre pour clavier majeure suivante, les *Valses nobles et sentimentales*, suscita donc le plus vif intérêt.

La SMI, dans la fondation de laquelle Ravel avait joué un rôle important, voulait s'opposer à ce que le compositeur considérait comme la rigidité et la pompe de la vie musicale française, et plus particulièrement des concerts de la Société nationale, où l'influence de Vincent d'Indy prédominait. La présence de *Ma mère l'Oye* au premier concert avait frappé un grand coup au nom de la liberté, de même que la décision, pour le treizième concert de la société, le 9 mai 1911, de jouer toutes les pièces anonymement, les noms des neuf compositeurs n'étant révélés qu'à la fin – et après que le public ait eu l'occasion de les deviner. Les *Valses* furent jouées par Louis Aubert, compositeur mineur, qui doit sans doute l'essentiel de sa renommée au fait que, dans son enfance, il chanta le « Pie Jesu » lors de la création du *Requiem* de Fauré. Bon nombre d'auditeurs attribuèrent correctement l'œuvre à Ravel, mais il y eut également des votes pour Satie et pour Kodály, entre autres. Il fut plus embarrassant pour Ravel d'avoir à essuyer les huées et les protestations [1], et d'entendre des amis intimes condamner ensuite les *Valses*, jugées peu musicales et même cacophoniques [2]. Il faut noter que, bien que la SMI ait continué d'exister jusqu'en 1935, cette expérience ne fut jamais renouvelée.

De façon générale, la faute n'incombe pas au public. Dans son esquisse autobiographique, Ravel évoque « une écriture nettement plus clarifiée, qui durcit l'harmonie et accuse les reliefs de la musique [3] ». Il fait également allusion à l'exemple de Schubert, dont les recueils de *Valses sentimentales* (D. 779, 1823) et de *Valses nobles* (D. 969, 1827) donnèrent ensemble à Ravel son titre – une influence qui semble être allée un peu plus loin que cela, encore que Roy Howat souligne que, au début de la première valse, Ravel emprunte le rythme de la première *Valse noble* de Schubert, mais en le décalant d'une noire, si bien que la levée de Schubert devient maintenant un temps fort [4].

Comme avec *Jeux d'eau*, Ravel place en tête de la partition une citation d'Henri de Régnier ; mais alors que dans la première œuvre l'épigraphe évoque le climat de la pièce, celle des *Valses nobles* semble tout le contraire d'une évocation : « Le plaisir délicieux et toujours nouveau d'une occupation inutile. » La danse, par essence « inutile », est, comme cette œuvre, sa propre justification. On peut pousser le parallèle plus loin. La tension entre les pas formels d'une danse et l'émotion des danseurs sur le parquet se reflète dans la tension entre les structures de phrase solidement contrôlées et leur contenu expressif, qui n'est pas toujours ce que l'on attend.

La violoniste Hélène Jourdan-Morhange, dans un entretien avec Vlado Perlemuter [5], attira l'attention sur le nombre exceptionnel d'indications « expressif » et « très expressif » dans la partition – quatorze en tout, dont cinq dans l'Épilogue.

Toutefois, la citation peut paraître plus objective lorsqu'on lit le roman de Régnier où elle est empruntée. *Les Rencontres de M. de Bréot*, publiées en 1904, sont l'histoire d'une « éducation sentimentale », au terme de laquelle le jeune M. de Bréot repense à ses aventures, de même que la dernière valse de l'œuvre de Ravel rappelle les précédentes :

> « Quand M. de Bréot songeait aux circonstances diverses de son séjour en une ville si fameuse par les aventures de toutes sortes qui y adviennent, il ne pouvait s'empêcher de constater qu'il n'y avait observé, pour sa part, que des événements assez ordinaires et aucun de ceux-là qui font de vous un autre homme. M. de Bréot était toujours M. de Bréot, pour lui-même comme pour les autres. Il pensait les mêmes choses qu'auparavant et n'en faisait guère de différentes. Il est vrai, pourtant, qu'il se mêlait en plus à ses pensées le souvenir de quelques personnages assez singuliers et qui valaient bien la peine, après tout, d'avoir quitté sa province pour la curiosité de leur connaissance et l'agrément de leur compagnie [6]. »

Une combinaison de « curiosité » et d'« agrément » : voilà une description tentante pour le style musical de Ravel en général, et celui des *Valses nobles* en particulier, où à ces qualités s'ajoutent les contraintes rythmiques de la danse. Harmoniquement, l'écriture, comme le dit Ravel, est d'une dureté nouvelle, après la somptuosité chatoyante d'œuvres comme « Ondine ». Celle-ci n'est pas tant le fait de « nouveaux » accords que de la présentation plus simple d'anciens ; jusqu'à l'Épilogue, où les « quelques personnages assez singuliers » des valses précédentes sont entrevus à travers les brumes du souvenir, il renonce dans une large mesure aux capacités évocatrices du piano. La tension dont il était question ci-dessus est en partie obtenue dans la première valse par l'entrelacs de gammes chromatiques avec le « cercle des quintes » à la basse qui progresse à travers les douze notes de la gamme ; et Ravel s'arrange pour que le retour du *ré* initial (à la mes. 61) coïncide avec le retour du matériau du début.

Les commentateurs citent souvent la texture bitonale de la section centrale de la septième valse, que Ravel considérait comme la plus caractéristique des *Valses* [7]. À ce stade de la carrière de Ravel, la bitonalité est toujours résolue et n'atteint pas l'indépendance contrapuntique qu'on trouve dans le *Duo* ou dans *L'Enfant et les sortilèges*. Un excellent exemple de ce genre de résolution, obtenue par la persistance, se trouve dans les trente-cinq dernières mesures de l'Épilogue, où la basse *sol* s'affirme contre tous les arrivants et a le dernier mot – merveilleuse fusion de technique et de poésie. Dans le roman, M. de Bréot et Mme de Brionne sont de même unis dans les dernières pages.

Les *Valses* n'ont jamais été la plus populaire des œuvres pour piano de Ravel, et on l'entendit même dire qu'elles étaient « maudites [8] ». En 1987, il s'en était vendu quelque 70 000 exemplaires, à comparer aux 120 000 du *Tombeau de Couperin* ou aux 250 000 de la *Sonatine*. Toutefois, 40 000 de ces 70 000 avaient été vendus depuis 1971, ce qui montre que les pianistes commençaient finalement à rattraper Ravel, mais avec soixante ans de retard [9]. La vérité est que les *Valses* sont très difficiles à bien jouer, posant de redoutables problèmes de pédale, d'indépendance des mains et – curieusement – de *rubato*, que Ravel avait normalement en horreur. Lorsque des phrases à 3/2 et à 3/4 sont présentes simultanément (mes. 7-10 de la première valse, par exemple), Ravel voulait que les deux rythmes soient audibles. Perlemuter raconte que Ravel lui fit répéter ces quatre mesures dix fois, les mains séparées, soulignant l'attitude du compositeur face à l'œuvre : « Je n'évoque pas sans une certaine émotion Ravel à son bureau, près du piano, partition en mains, me faisant travailler ces *Valses*. Je n'avais jamais vu tant d'acuité dans son regard, il y avait chez lui un tel désir d'être compris, de ne rien laisser passer non seulement dans son texte, mais dans l'interprétation de ce texte. Par le désir de perfection de la lettre, on rejoignait, involontairement, l'esprit [10]. »

L'expérience d'Henriette Faure fut comparable : « Il se leva, se tint près du piano et m'infligea un supplice qu'un demi-siècle n'arrive pas à me faire oublier, m'arrêtant continuellement, me reprenant dans les moindres détails, pour une respiration, un silence, une pédale, une inflexion... et au fond de tout cela, comme une horloge au fond d'un couloir ses inexorables 1 2 3, 1 2 3... C'était épuisant, il fallait intégrer la fantaisie dans la rigueur et donner du rêve ou de l'élégance dans le maximum de rythme et de précision. Ce martyre dura près de deux heures et demie [11]. »

Certains des commentaires plus généraux de Perlemuter et de Faure sur les valses individuelles méritent d'être notés ici (leurs remarques sur des mesures ou des phrases particulières sont reproduites dans le commentaire critique) :

I  « Il faut de la force, du son, mais pas de dureté » (**PerS** 43). Cette valse « fait alterner le percutant, et les vagues de legato expressif » (**FauS** 39).

II  « Ravel ne trouvait jamais assez extérieur ce soufflet » (**PerS** 44).

III  « La difficulté de cette valse est de bien isoler le troisième temps, cela donne une hésitation avant d'aborder le premier temps [de la mesure suivante] » (**PerS** 44). « La troisième petite mécanique précise, ciselée, où alternent les passages qui demandent un petit mouvement sec et court du poignet et des doigts d'acier nuance pianissimo, et des phrasés d'un legato expressif et ondulant. Là aussi toujours le rythme absolu laissant apparaître très passagèrement quelques petits ralentis expressifs mais que l'auteur voulait très courts et aussitôt rentrés dans l'ordre » (**FauS** 39).

IV  « Comme toujours, Ravel voulait le soufflet très marqué, mais sans s'attarder » (**PerS** 46).

V  La partition de Perlemuter porte l'inscription manuscrite : « Dans l'esprit d'une valse de Schubert ». Mais elle n'est pas, comme il le prétend, de la main de Ravel, bien que le compositeur l'ait très probablement dictée. Il en va de même d'autres annotations, dont **PerS** affirme aussi qu'elles sont de Ravel. « Dans le travail, Ravel m'avez suggéré le titre de "Valse Vénitienne" pour aider au style romantique. Ravel voulait cette valse comme une poupée en soie et velours ; il m'avez suggéré le titre de "Valse 1830" » (**FauS** 40-41).

VI  Ici encore, Perlemuter souligne l'importance qu'il y a à faire ressortir les rythmes binaires à la main gauche : « C'est le seul moyen d'arriver à mater ce passage et de le réussir comme l'exigeait Ravel » (**PerS** 50).

VII  Voir le commentaire critique pour les détails.

VIII – Épilogue  « Ravel tenait tellement à cette unité de mouvement qu'il faut y insister. C'est d'ailleurs une des difficultés d'interprétation de cette valse... Ravel voulait que l'Épilogue fût lent mais qu'il gardât son rythme de valse » (**PerS** 53-54).

En l'espace de quinze jours seulement, en mars 1912, Ravel orchestra les *Valses* pour former le ballet *Adélaïde ou le Langage des fleurs*. L'impresario responsable de cette entreprise était Jacques Rouché, qui venait de mettre en scène le ballet *Ma mère l'Oye* à son Théâtre des Arts à la fin de janvier. Le ballet de Ravel formait une quadruple affiche au Théâtre du Châtelet le 22 avril, avec *La Péri* de Dukas (dont c'était également la création), *La Tragédie de Salomé* de Schmitt et *Istar* de d'Indy. Chaque compositeur dirigea sa propre composition, et la soirée était intitulée *Concert de danse, N. Trouhanowa* – la ballerine qui apparaissait dans chaque œuvre. La première audition en concert de la version orchestrale fut donnée le 15 février 1914, sous la direction de Pierre Monteux [12].

On pense généralement que cette transcription orchestrale est l'une des réalisations les plus étonnantes de Ravel. La tentation pour l'éditeur est donc de reprendre dans la version pour piano seul toutes les indications de la partition orchestrale. Mais un message autographe provenant des effets de Ravel [13] nous met en garde de façon générale : « Nuances, accents, points, liaisons peuvent et doivent souvent être différents dans la transposition d'orchestre ». Le mot-clef est ici « souvent ». Malgré l'avertissement de Ravel, il y a quelques endroits où la partition d'orchestre (**RO**) offre une aide incontestable à l'interprète, et ces passages sont dûment référencés dans le commentaire critique. De toute façon, seul un professeur insensible pourrait activement dissuader ses élèves d'écouter les orchestrations magiques de Ravel.

### Principes d'édition

Tous les ajouts de l'éditeur sont entre crochets. Les parenthèses indiquent des variantes provenant de sources secondaires, dont les détails sont donnés dans le commentaire critique, ou des altérations de précaution provenant de **AM** et de **E** ; il y a également une unique altération de précaution à la mes. 58 de l'Épilogue. Les doigtés sont de Ravel, et proviennent de **AM** ou de **CE**, comme indiqué dans le commentaire critique.

Les indications de pédale dans **AM**, reproduites dans **E**, sont rares : deux dans la Valse II, et un certain nombre d'indications « 3 cordes » et « sourdine » dans l'Épilogue. On pourrait être tenté de tirer des indications de pédale de **RR**. Toutefois, non seulement Ravel était un pianiste médiocre (comme en témoigne en particulier son interprétation de la Valse I), mais son enregistrement de 1913 était sa première rencontre avec cette technique, et il est communément admis que, dans les situations tendues, la pédale est l'une des premières choses à souffrir. Les indications dans **GarCP** ne coïncident que partiellement avec ce qu'on relève dans **RR**. Comme il n'y a pas d'indications de pédale supplémentaires dans **CE**, où Ravel aurait eu toute latitude pour les introduire, il semble en général que le mieux soit de laisser la pédalisation à la discrétion de l'interprète. Des exceptions sont faites aux endroits où Perlemuter ou Faure ont des indications particulières à transmettre, ou lorsque la pédalisation dans **RR** est intéressante sans être affectée par les déficiences techniques de Ravel : dans ces cas, les indications sont données dans le commentaire critique.

### Table des abréviations des sources

**AM** : autographe sur microfilm

**E** : première édition, publiée par Durand, déposée à la BnF le 28 décembre 1911 (D&F. 8247)

**CE** : exemplaire corrigé de la première édition de Ravel

**CasCE** : exemplaire imprimé avec les additions et corrections de Casadesus

**GarCP** : épreuve imprimée avec additions et corrections de Garban

**GarT** : transcription pour piano à quatre mains de Garban, publiée par Durand en 1918 (D&F. 9549)

**PerCE** : exemplaire imprimé de Perlemuter avec additions et corrections de Ravel

**RO** : transcription orchestrale de Ravel, publiée par Durand en 1912 (D&F. 8476)

**RR** : enregistrement de Ravel sur rouleau de piano

**CasR** : enregistrement de Casadesus

**FévR** : enregistrement de Février

**PerRI** et **PerRII** : enregistrements de Perlemuter (la mention **PerR** sans chiffre indique que les deux enregistrements de Perlemuter coïncident sur le point en question)

**PerS** : souvenirs de Perlemuter dans *Ravel d'après Ravel*, entretiens avec Hélène Jourdan-Morhange

**FauS** : souvenirs d'Henriette Faure, dans *Mon maître Maurice Ravel*

*Roger Nichols*
2007
Traduction : Dennis Collins

---

[1] « Esquisse autobiographique », *La Revue musicale* (décembre 1938), 21.

[2] Louis Aubert à Manuel Rosenthal, qui nous le rapporta dans une conservation.

[3] Voir note 1, *ibid.*

[4] R. Howat, *The Piano music of Debussy, Ravel, Fauré and Chabrier : explorations and illuminations*, Yale, 2008, ch. 17 (je remercie l'auteur de m'avoir permis de consulter le tapuscrit de ce livre).

[5] PerS 44.

[6] *Les Rencontres de M. de Bréot*, Paris, Mercure de France, 1904, 272-273.

[7] Voir note 1, *ibid.*

[8] Roland-Manuel, cité dans **FauS** 37.

[9] Je remercie la maison Durand de m'avoir donné accès à ces chiffres.

[10] PerS 42.

[11] FauS 20.

[12] Pour plus de renseignements, voir Deborah Mawer, *The Ballets of Maurice Ravel*, Aldershot, Ashgate, 2006, 125-148.

[13] Contenu sur un microfilm de la BnF, Vm. micr. 860.

# RAVELS KLAVIERMUSIK – NEUE AUSGABE
## Editorische Methode und Quellen

Es ist nicht zu leugnen, dass sich ein Gefühl der Aufregung einstellt, wenn man die autographe Handschrift eines musikalischen Meisterwerks in Händen hält, und wenn darüber hinaus das Autograph selbst ein Kunstwerk ist, wie bei Ravel oft der Fall, so wird dieses Gefühl durch ästhetische Eindrücke noch verstärkt. Ebenso wenig ist jedoch zu leugnen, dass Komponisten wie alle Sterblichen fehlbar sind, und dass das Autograph, so schön und aufregend es sein mag, Fehler enthalten kann. Das scheinbar löbliche Unterfangen, auf das zurückzugreifen, was der Komponist ursprünglich schrieb, muss daher mit einer gewissen Portion Allgemeinverstand aufgewogen werden.

Bei Bühnenwerken führen zeitliche, räumliche, finanzielle und persönliche Zwänge ohne Frage oft zu Eingriffen, die der Komponist in keiner Weise begrüßt, die er aber billigen muss, will er die Aufführung nicht gefährden, und die so in die gedruckte Partitur gelangen. Im Falle von Klavierwerken ist der Druck auf den Komponisten bei der Vorbereitung einer Ausgabe jedoch wesentlich geringer (und wird vor allem vom Verleger ausgeübt, der den Verlagsrichtlinien zu entsprechen sucht), so dass Änderungen auf dem Wege von der Handschrift zur Druckausgabe mit größerer Wahrscheinlichkeit dem Willen des Komponisten entsprechen. Natürlich können im Verlauf der Drucklegung Fehler sowohl entstehen als auch korrigiert werden, und wenn allgemeine und musikalische Erwägungen dies vermuten lassen, kann sich das Autograph tatsächlich oft als ein wichtiges Indiz erweisen. In Gesprächen mit zahlreichen Komponisten der Gegenwart aber wurde mir ganz überwiegend versichert, dass sie vielmehr verärgert wären, würden zukünftige Herausgeber ihre sorgsam erarbeiteten gedruckten Partituren übergehen und auf der Suche nach einer angeblich korrekten Lesart automatisch auf ihre originalen Manuskripte zurückgreifen.

Im Falle von Ravels Klaviermusik ist ein solch kritischer Umgang mit handschriftlichen Zeugnissen mehr denn je gerechtfertigt, findet sich doch in der Musikabteilung der Bibliothèque Nationale de France eine gebundene Sammlung von Ravels eigenen Exemplaren fast aller gedruckten Erstausgaben seiner Solowerke für Klavier samt autographer Korrekturen[1]. Dem Inhalt nach zu urteilen wurde der Band wohl zwischen 1911 und 1913 zusammengestellt. Bei den fehlenden Werken handelt es sich um die *Sérénade grotesque*, *Sites auriculaires*, *Ma mère l'oye*, *Prélude*, *A la manière de...*, *Le tombeau de Couperin* und *Frontispice*. Gedruckte Ausgaben von *Ma mère l'oye* und *A la manière de...* mit autographen Korrekturen finden sich an anderem Ort in derselben Bibliothek[2], während Ravels eigenes Druckexemplar von *Le tombeau de Couperin* mit eigenhändigen Fingersätzen und einer einzigen autographen Korrektur im Musée Ravel in Montfort l'Amaury ausgestellt ist. Bei der *Sérénade grotesque* und *Sites auriculaires* können die Autographen als vorrangige Quellen betrachtet werden, da diese Werke nicht zu Lebzeiten des Komponisten veröffentlicht wurden. Die Eigenschrift von *Frontispice* ist ebenfalls von Bedeutung, da Ravels eigene gedruckte Ausgabe verschollen ist. Für *Prélude* liegt leider weder das Autograph noch das Druckexemplar des Komponisten vor.

Nach aktuellem Kenntnisstand existieren keine Korrekturabzüge der Erstausgaben von Ravels Klavierwerken außer einem Satz Erstkorrekturfahnen von *Le tombeau de Couperin* im Archiv von Durand, die von einem Durand-Lektor berichtet und mit einer Bitte um Zweitkorrekturabzüge versehen wurden. (Herzlich möchte ich Roy Howat danken, der mir eine Kopie dieses Materials zur Verfügung stellte.) Dieser Satz enthält keine autographen Eintragungen. Sämtliche Korrekturanweisungen wurden in der Erstausgabe berücksichtigt, mit Ausnahme der Gestaltung einiger Mehrfach-Vorschläge in „Prélude" und „Forlane" von *Le tombeau de Couperin*, bezüglich derer augenscheinlich Ravel seine Meinung änderte.

### Hauptquellen

Wo Ravels eigenes korrigiertes Exemplar verfügbar war, wurde dieses als Hauptquelle zugrunde gelegt; Abweichungen zwischen dieser korrigierten Ausgabe (**CE**), der gedruckten Erstausgabe (**E**) und dem Autograph sind entsprechend vermerkt. Das neunseitige Autograph der *Valses nobles* (in der Sammlung Taverne) ist zu Forschungszwecken bislang nicht zugänglich, doch existiert ein Mikrofilm (**AM**) in der Musikabteilung der Bibliothèque nationale de France (Vm. micr. 876).

### Nebenquellen

Die Nebenquellen gliedern sich in vier Gruppen:

(a) Druckexemplare mit Korrekturen von Musikern aus Ravels Umfeld

(I) Ausgaben von Ravels Klavierwerken aus dem Besitz von Robert Casadesus (**CasCE**), nunmehr ebenfalls in der Musikabteilung der BNF verwahrt; sein Exemplar der *Valses nobles* findet sich unter der Signatur Vm. Casadesus 940. Es enthält keine Eintragungen von Hand des Komponisten.

(II) Einige Exemplare, unter anderem jenes der *Valses nobles*, aus dem Besitz von Vlado Perlemuter (**PerCE**), nun ebenfalls im Bestand der BNF, jedoch bisher nicht katalogisiert.

(III) Einige Exemplare mit Korrekturen von Lucien Garban. Garban arbeitete für den Verlag Durand und war ein enger Freund des Komponisten. Der genaue Rang dieser Korrekturen ist nicht festzustellen, doch angesichts der Verbindung der beiden ist es denkbar, dass zumindest ein Teil der Änderungen auf Ravel zurückgeht. Diese Exemplare befinden sich nun in der der Bibliothek des Bakersfield College in Kalifornien. Garban bearbeitete darüber hinaus die *Valses nobles et sentimentales* sowie *Le tombeau de Couperin* für Klavier zu vier Händen. Diese Transkriptionen werden bei Durand verlegt.

(IV) Zu den Ausgaben, die nicht herangezogen wurden, gehören jene aus dem Besitz von Jacques Février, dessen Nichte und Schülerin Mme Aboulker-Rosenfeld mir versicherte, dass sie über seine Fingersätze hinaus keine Eintragungen enthielten, sowie jene von Henriette Faure, die verschollen sind.

(b) Ravels eigene Orchestrierungen etlicher seiner Klavierstücke (**RO**). In chronologischer Reihenfolge der Erstkomposition (Jahr der Orchestrierung in Klammern) umfassen diese: das *Menuet antique* (1929), die „Habanera" aus *Sites auriculaires* (1908), *Pavane pour une Infante défunte* (1910), „Une barque sur l'océan" und „Alborada del gracioso" aus den *Miroirs* (1906 und 1923), *Ma mère l'oye* (1911), *Valses nobles et sentimentales* (1912) sowie „Prélude", „Forlane", „Menuet" und „Rigaudon" aus *Le tombeau de Couperin* (1919).

(c) Einspielungen

(I) Klavierrollen, die Ravel 1913 für Welte-Mignon einspielte (*Sonatine*, 1. und 2. Satz, C2887; *Valses nobles et sentimentales*, C2888) und 1922 für Duo-Art (*Pavane pur une Infante défunte*, 084; „Oiseaux tristes" aus den *Miroirs*, 082). Es ist behauptet worden, dass Ravel bei dieser zweiten Gelegenheit auch „Le gibet" aus *Gaspard de la nuit* und die „Toccata" aus *Le tombeau de Couperin* aufgenommen habe, doch wurden diese vielmehr von Robert Casadesus aufgezeichnet. Es bleibt fraglich, welcher der beiden 1929 für Duo-Art „La vallée des cloches" aus *Miroirs* einspielte (72750), obwohl der Herausgeber sich nahezu sicher ist, dass es Ravel war. All diese Einspielungen sind verschiedentlich auf LP übertragen worden, doch leider war die Klavierrollen-Wiedergabe dabei nicht immer optimal eingestellt.

(II) Schallplattenaufnahmen dreier Pianisten, die sämtlich in den Genuss genauer Anweisungen vom Komponisten kamen: Robert Casadesus (1955, CBS 13062-4[3]); Jacques Février (1972, ADES 7041-4); Vlado Perlemuter (1961, VOX VBX 410 1-3[4]; 1977, NIMBUS 2101-3, später erschienen als CD NI 5005, 5011). Marcelle Meyer war zwar mit Ravel bekannt (sie gaben zusammen jene Privataufführung von *La valse* auf zwei Klavieren, welche Diaghilev bekanntermaßen unbeeindruckt ließ), doch studierte sie seine Klavierwerke nie mit ihm ein, wie mir ihre Tochter Marie Bertin freundlicherweise mitteilte. Ich habe daher Mme Meyers Ravel-Aufnahmen, die von EMI beim Label Référence neu veröffentlicht wurden, außer Acht gelassen.

(d) Erinnerungen an Ravel als Vermittler seiner Klaviermusik

(I) von Vlado Perlemuter in seinen Interviews mit Hélène Jourdan-Morhange, veröffentlicht als *Ravel d'après Ravel* (Lausanne 1953) sowie in englischer Übersetzung als *Ravel according to Ravel* (New York/London 1988; 2/1991)[5].

(II) von Vlado Perlemuter im Gespräch mit dem Herausgeber der vorliegenden Ausgabe.

(III) von Henriette Faure in *Mon maître Maurice Ravel* (Paris 1978) (**FauS**). Mlle Faure, die Schwester des Politikers Edgar Faure, nahm anlässlich ihres Recitals seiner Musik im Theâtre des Champs-Elysées am 12. Januar 1923 (nicht am 18. Januar, wie in ihrem Buch behauptet) – wahrscheinlich das erste Recital überhaupt, das ausschließlich Ravel gewidmet war – im Alter von 18 Jahren Unterricht beim Komponisten. Ihre Tochter, Mme Mayette Constantin, teilte mir freundlicherweise mit, dass sie einst im Besitz der originalen Aufzeichnungen ihrer Mutter gewesen sei, die unmittelbar auf Ravels Anweisungen beruhten, dass sie diese jedoch einem Forscher zur Verfügung gestellt und nie zurückerhalten habe. Auf andere Erinnerungen wird an Ort und Stelle verwiesen.

Die Nebenquellen sind immer dort einbezogen, wo sie zusätzliche Erkenntnisse über die etablierte Lesart vermitteln oder wo Probleme des Notentextes nicht anhand der Hauptquellen gelöst werden konnten.

### Danksagungen

Ich danke den folgenden Personen für ihre freundliche Unterstützung: Gaby Casadesus für Informationen über ihren Gatten Robert; Dr. Michel Noiray, der mich auf das Autograph der *Sonatine* aufmerksam machte und mir bei der Beschaffung einer Kopie behilflich war; James Segesta, Bibliothekar beim Leserdienst des California State College in Bakersfield, der mir Kopien der korrigierten Exemplare von Lucien Garban zusandte; Jean Touzelet, und später Denis Hall und Rex Lawson, die es mir ermöglichten, Ravels Duo-Art-Klavierrollen auf einwandfrei funktionierenden Geräten anzuhören; und Dr. J. Rigbie Turner, Leiter der Abteilung für Musikhandschriften und –bücher in der Piepont Morgan Library in New York, für die Zusendung von Kopien der Autographen von *Jeux d'Eau* sowie von „Noctuelles" und „Oiseaux tristes" aus *Miroirs*. Darüber hinaus bin ich verschiedenen ausübenden Musikern zu Dank verpflichtet: Vlado Perlemuter, der mit mir über seinen Unterricht bei Ravel sprach und es mir gestattete, seine Notenausgaben durchzusehen; Roy Howat für seine Ratschläge, die stets Wissenschaft und Praxis zu vereinbaren wussten; Junko Okazaki, der mir eine Fotokopie von Perlemuters Exemplar der *Valses nobles* zur Verfügung stellte; sowie Michael Channon, Anthony Goldstone und Charles Timbrell für ihre Ansichten zum Tamtam in „Laideronette" und anderen Einzelheiten in *Ma mère l'oye*. Schließlich danke ich den Mitarbeitern der Musikabteilung der Bibliothèque Nationale sowie Margaret Cobb, Graham Hayter, Olivier Mazal, Gwendolyn Mok, Jean-Michel Nectoux, Dr. Arbie Orenstein und Dr. Stephen Roe für zahlreiche freundliche Hilfeleistungen.

---

[1] Ursprünglich Vma. 2967, nunmehr unter der Signatur Rés. Vma. 493.

[2] Vma. 3157(7) bzw. Fol. Vm12. 2701(2)A

[3] Später erschienen als SONY MH2K 63316.

[4] Später erschienen als VOX CDX2 5507.

[5] Doppelte Seitenangaben beziehen sich jeweils auf die französische und englische Ausgabe.

# VALSES NOBLES ET SENTIMENTALES

## Vorwort

Mit der Uraufführung von *Gaspard de la nuit* durch Ricardo Viñes am 9. Januar 1909 in der Salle Erard in Paris etablierte sich Ravel ein für alle Mal als bedeutender Komponist und räumte mit dem hartnäckigen Vorurteil auf, er sei lediglich ein Abklatsch Debussys. Die Vorstellung seines nächsten Klavierwerks, *Ma mère l'oye,* beim Gründungskonzert der Société Musicale Indépendante (SMI) am 20. April 1910 trug jedoch zunächst kaum zur Festigung dieser Stellung bei – einige jener, die in ihm einen Hoffnungsträger gesehen hatten, zeigten sich vielmehr enttäuscht. Zweifellos war man daher überaus gespannt zu hören, was sein nächstes großes Klavierwerk bringen würde, die *Valses nobles et sentimentales*.

Zweck der SMI, bei deren Gründung Ravel eine führende Rolle gespielt hatte, war es, der Langeweile und Aufgeblasenheit entgegenzuwirken, die seiner Wahrnehmung nach das französische Musikleben und speziell die Konzerte der Société Nationale prägten, welche mittlerweile unter dem vorwiegenden Einfluss Vincent d'Indys stand. *Ma mère* auf das Programm des ersten Konzertes zu setzen, war ein Befreiungsschlag gewesen, und ein ebensolcher war die Idee, sämtliche Stücke beim 13. Konzert der Gesellschaft am 9. Mai 1911 anonym zu spielen und die Namen der neun Komponisten erst am Ende preiszugeben – nachdem das Publikum Gelegenheit zur Spekulation gehabt hatte. Die *Valses* wurden von Louis Aubert gespielt, einem unbedeutenden Komponisten, der sich musikgeschichtlich wohl eher dadurch hervortat, dass er als Knabe das „Pie Jesu" in der Uraufführung von Faurés *Requiem* sang. Etliche errieten Ravel, es fielen jedoch unter anderem auch die Namen Satie und Kodály. Unangenehmer war es für Ravel, dass er sich Proteste und Zwischenrufe anhören musste[1] und enge Freunde des Komponisten das Werk unmittelbar im Anschluss als unmusikalisch und sogar als übeltönend verurteilten[2]. Obwohl die SMI bis 1935 bestand, wurde das Experiment bezeichnenderweise nie wiederholt.

Das Publikum trifft aus heutiger Sicht nur geringe Schuld. In seiner autobiographischen Skizze spricht Ravel von einem „Stil, der einfacher und deutlicher ist, in dem der Zusammenklang schärfer ist und die musikalischen Linien hervortreten"[3]. Er führt darüber hinaus das Beispiel Schubert an, dessen Sammlungen *Valses sentimentales* (D 779, 1823) und *Valses nobles* (D 969, 1827) zusammen Ravel seinen Titel lieferten – worin sich der Einfluss jedoch auch schon zu erschöpfen scheint, obgleich Roy Howat darauf hingewiesen hat, dass Ravel zu Beginn der ersten Valse den Rhythmus von Schuberts erster *Valse noble* übernahm, ihn aber um ein Viertel nach hinten verschob, so dass Schuberts Auftakt nun auf eine betonte Zählzeit fällt[4].

Wie bei *Jeux d'eau* stellt Ravel dem Notentext ein Zitat Henri de Régniers voran, doch während der Dichterspruch dort auf den Charakter des Stückes einstimmt, scheint die Überschrift der *Valses nobles* ihm genau entgegengesetzt: „le plaisir délicieux et toujours nouveau d'une occupation inutile" („das köstliche und stets neue Vergnügen eines müßigen Zeitvertreibs"). Tanzen ist im Wesentlichen „müßig" und, wie das vorliegende Stück, sich selbst genug. Der Vergleich kann noch weiter geführt werden. Die Spannung zwischen den festgelegten Schritten eines Tanzes und den Emotionen der Tanzenden spiegelt sich in der Spannung zwischen der exakt regulierten Phrasengestaltung und ihrem Ausdrucksgehalt, der unseren Erwartungen mitunter zuwiderläuft. Die Geigerin Hélène Jourdan-Morhange hat im Gespräch mit Vlado Perlemuter[5] diesbezüglich auf das ungewöhnlich häufige Vorkommen der Vortragsbezeichnungen „expressif" und „très expressif" im Notentext hingewiesen – 14 Mal insgesamt, fünfmal davon im Epilog.

Das Zitat erscheint jedoch um einiges objektiver, wenn man den Roman Régniers liest, dem es entstammt. *Les rencontres de M. de Bréot*, 1904 erschienen, ist die Geschichte einer „Gefühlsbildung", an deren Ende der junge M. de Bréot auf seine Abenteuer zurückblickt, ganz wie die letzte Valse des Ravelschen Werks auf die vorhergehenden zurückverweist:

> „wenn M. de Bréot an die verschiedenen Dinge dachte, die sich während seines Aufenthalts in Paris ereignet hatten, einer Stadt, die dafür berühmt war, dass sie alle möglichen Erfahrungen bot, gelangte er zwangsläufig zu dem Schluss, dass er für seinen Teil ausschließlich gewöhnliche Begebenheiten beobachtet hatte und keine von der Art, die einen zu einem neuen Menschen machen. M. de Bréot war immer noch M. de Bréot, für sich selbst wie für jedermann sonst. Er dachte die gleichen Gedanken wie zuvor und verrichtete die gleichen Tätigkeiten. Dennoch verweilten seine Gedanken durchaus auch bei der Erinnerung an verschiedene recht ungewöhnliche Gestalten, die es letzten Endes lohnend erscheinen ließen, die Provinz verlassen zu haben, dank der Interessantheit (*curiosité*) ihrer Bekanntschaft und der Angenehmheit (*agrément*) ihrer Gesellschaft."[6]

Eine Verbindung von „curiosité" und „agrément" bietet sich auch als treffende Beschreibung von Ravels musikalischem Stil im Allgemeinen und der *Valses nobles* im Besonderen an, bei denen zu diesen Eigenschaften noch die rhythmischen Maßgaben des Tanzes hinzutreten. Harmonisch ist der Stil nach der schillernden Opulenz solcher Stücke wie „Ondine" von einer, wie Ravel sagt, neuen Schärfe geprägt. Diese rührt nicht so sehr von „neuen" Akkorden her als von der schmucklosen Gestaltung der alten, und bis zum Epilog, in dem sich der Blick durch den Nebel der Erinnerung auf die „verschiedenen recht ungewöhnlichen Gestalten" der vorhergehenden Walzer zurückwendet, wird das atmosphärische Potenzial des Klaviers kaum ausgeschöpft. Die oben erwähnte Spannung wird in der ersten Valse durch die Verflechtung von chromatischen Skalen und dem „Quintenzirkel" im Bass erreicht, der alle zwölf Töne der Skala durchschreitet, und Ravel lässt die Wiederkehr des anfänglichen D (in Takt 61) mit der Wiederaufnahme der Eingangsmotivik zusammenfallen.

Zahlreiche Autoren haben auf die bitonale Struktur im Mittelteil des siebten Walzers hingewiesen, den Ravel für den typischsten der *Valses* erachtete[7]. In dieser Phase des Ravelschen Stils erfährt Bitonalität stets eine Auflösung und erlangt keine kontrapunktische Selbständigkeit, wie sie im *Duo* oder in *L'Enfant et les sortilèges* zu finden ist. Ein hervorragendes Beispiel für diese Art der Auflösung nach langem Beharren findet sich in den letzten 35 Takten des Epilogs, in denen das G im Bass sich gegen alle Emporkömmlinge durchsetzt und das letzte Wort hat – eine wunderbare Verschmelzung von Technik und Poesie. Auch im Roman finden M. de Bréot und Mme De Brionne auf den letzten Seiten schließlich zusammen.

Die *Valses* gehörten nie zu den beliebtesten der Ravelschen Klavierwerke, und von ihm selbst ist gar die Äußerung überliefert, sie seien „maudites" (verflucht)[8]. Bis 1987 hatten sich 70.000 Exemplare verkauft, im Vergleich zu 120.000 von *Le tombeau de Couperin* oder 250.000 der *Sonatine*. Jedoch gingen 40.000 dieser 70.000 nach 1971 über den Ladentisch, was darauf hindeutet, dass die Pianisten schließlich den Anschluss an Ravel fanden, wenn auch erst nach 60 Jahren[9]. Tatsache ist, dass die *Valses* nur sehr schwer befriedigend zu spielen sind und gefürchtete Anforderungen stellen im Hinblick auf Pedalgebrauch, Unabhängigkeit der Hände und merkwürdigerweise auch auf das *rubato*, das Ravel für gewöhnlich ein Greuel war. Wo Phrasen im 3/2- und 3/4-Takt gleichzeitig erklingen (etwa in Takt 7-10 der ersten Valse), beharrte Ravel darauf, dass beide Rhythmen hörbar zu sein hätten. Perlemuter entsinnt sich, dass Ravel ihn diese vier Takte zehnmal hintereinander wiederholen ließ, mit getrennten Händen, und bemerkt zum Verhältnis des Komponisten zu diesem Werk: „Ich erinnere mich mit einer gewissen Ergriffenheit an den Anblick Ravels, wie er am Schreibtisch neben dem Klavier saß, die Noten in der Hand, und mir diese *Valses* erläuterte. Ich hatte seine Augen nie so leuchten sehen – er war so entschlossen, sich verständlich zu machen, nichts in den Noten oder, in gleichem Maße, in ihrer Interpretation zu übergehen. Durch diese Leidenschaft zur textlichen Perfektion fand man sich automatisch auch geistig eingestimmt."[10]

Henriette Faures Erfahrung war ähnlich: „Er stand auf, stellte sich neben das Klavier und unterzog mich einer Tortur, die ich auch nach einem halben Jahrhundert nicht vergessen habe, er unterbrach mich fortlaufend, monierte geringste Feinheiten meines Spiels, eine Zäsur, eine Pause, einen Pedalgebrauch, einen Tonfall… und hinter alledem, wie eine Uhr am Ende des Korridors, sein unerbittliches 1 2 3 1 2 3… Es war strapaziös, man musste Fantasie mit Strenge verbinden und Träumerei und Eleganz bei äußerster Rhythmik und Präzision erzielen. Diese Martyrium währte fast zweieinhalb Stunden."[11]

Einige allgemeinere Kommentare Perlemuters und Faures zu den einzelnen Valses sind es wert, hier festgehalten zu werden (ihre Anmerkungen zu einzelnen Takten oder Phrasen sind im Kritischen Bericht verzeichnet):

I „Kraft und Klangfülle sind erforderlich, nicht aber Härte." (**PerS** 43/44) Dieser Walzer „wechselt zwischen perkussiven Passagen und Wellen ausdrucksvollen Legatos". (**FauS** 39)

II Zu den Dynamik-„Gabeln" in diesem Walzer heißt es: „Ravel fand sie nie ausreichend betont." (**PerS** 44/46)

III „Die Schwierigkeit besteht bei dieser dritten Valse darin, den dritten Schlag zu isolieren; dies bewirkt ein Zögern, bevor man den ersten Schlag [des folgenden Taktes] spielt." (**PerS** 44/46) „Die dritte Valse ist ein winziger, präziser, fein geschliffener Mechanismus, mit einem Wechsel zwischen Passagen, die kurze, heftige Bewegungen des Handgelenks und stahlharte Finger bei gleichzeitigem Pianissimo verlangen, und ausdrucksvollen, wogenden Legatophrasen. Auch hier muss der Rhythmus äußerst präzise sein und nur ganz flüchtig Raum lassen für vereinzelte behutsame, expressive Rallentandi, die Ravel aber sehr kurz wünschte sofort wieder unter Kontrolle gebracht wissen wollte." (**FauS** 39)

IV „Wie gewohnt wollte Ravel, dass man die Dynamik-Gabeln betone, ohne dabei jedoch langsamer zu werden." (**PerS** 46/48)

V Perlemuters Notentext ist mit der handschriftlichen Eintragung „Dans l'esprit d'une Valse de Schubert" überschrieben. Sie stammt jedoch nicht, wie er behauptet, von Ravels Hand, auch wenn sie mit großer Sicherheit auf ihn zurückgeht. Gleiches gilt für weitere Anmerkungen, von denen in **PerS** ebenfalls behauptet wird, sie stammten von Ravel. „Als wir daran arbeiteten, schlug Ravel den Titel ‚Venezianischer Walzer' vor, um das Romantische des Stils zu verdeutlichen. Ravel stellte sich diese Valse wie eine Puppe aus Samt und Seide vor; er legte mir den Titel ‚Valse 1830' nahe." (**FauS** 40f.)

VI Auch hier betonte Perlemuter wiederum die Wichtigkeit, die

Zweierrhythmen der linken Hand hervorzuheben: „Nur so gewinnt diese Passage Zusammenhalt und erlangt die von Ravel verlangte Qualität." (**PerS** 50/52)

VII  Nähere Angaben vgl. Kritischer Bericht.

VIII – Epilog  „Ravel lag die Einheit des Tempos hier so am Herzen, dass ich darauf bestehen muss. Sie ist zudem eine der Schwierigkeiten bei der Aufführung dieser Valse. [...] Ravel wollte, dass der Epilog langsam ist, dabei aber seinen Walzerrhythmus behält." (**PerS** 53f./56f.)

Innerhalb von nur zwei Wochen orchestrierte Ravel die *Valses* im März 1912 und schuf so das Ballett *Adélaïde ou le langue des fleurs*. Der Impresario, auf den diese Unternehmung zurückging, war Jacques Roché, der Ende Januar gerade die Ballettfassung von *Ma mère l'oye* an seinem Théâtre des Arts dirigiert hatte. Ravels Ballett wurde im Rahmen eines vierteiligen Programms am 22. April gemeinsam mit Dukas' *La Péri* (ebenfalls einer Premiere), Schmitts *La Tragédie de Salomé* und d'Indys *Istar* am Châtelet-Theater aufgeführt. Alle Komponisten dirigierten ihre Werke selbst, und das Ereignis wurde als *Concert de la danse, N. Trouhanowa* angekündigt – unter dem Namen jener Ballerina, die in allen vier Werken in Erscheinung trat. Die Konzertpremiere der Orchesterfassung fand am 15. Februar 1914 unter der Leitung von Pierre Monteux statt[12].

Diese Transkription für Orchester gilt weithin als eine der erstaunlichsten Schöpfungen Ravels. Als Herausgeber steht man daher vor der Versuchung, sämtliche Vortragsbezeichnungen aus der Orchesterpartitur in den Notentext für Klavier zurück zu übertragen. Eine handschriftliche Mitteilung aus Ravels Nachlass[13] enthält jedoch den grundsätzlichen Hinweis: „nuances accents points liaisons peuvent et doivent souvent être différents dans la transposition d'orchestre" („Nuancen, Akzente, Punkte, Bindebögen können und müssen in der Orchesterbearbeitung oft anders sein"). Das Schlüsselwort ist dabei „oft". Ravels Warnung zum Trotz liefert die Orchesterpartitur (**RO**) an einigen Stellen zweifellos Anhaltspunkte für die Interpretation, und auf diese Stellen wird im Kritischen Bericht entsprechend verwiesen. Es wäre jener jedenfalls ein hartherziger Lehrer, der seinen Schülern davon abriete, Ravels zauberhaften Orchestrierungen zu lauschen.

### Editorische Richtlinien

Alle Zusätze des Herausgebers sind durch eckige Klammern gekennzeichnet. Runde Klammern bezeichnen entweder Lesarten in den Nebenquellen, in welchem Falle nähere Angaben im Kritischen Bericht zu finden sind, oder Warnungsakzidenzien aus **AM** und **E**; ein einziges Warnungsakzidenz des Herausgebers erscheint in Takt 58 des Epilogs. Fingersätze stammen von Ravel und sind entweder aus **AM** oder **CE** übernommen, wie im Kritischen Bericht vermerkt.

Es existieren nur vereinzelte Pedalangaben in **AM**, die **E** übernimmt: zwei in Valse II sowie mehrfach die Anweisungen *3 cordes* und *sourdine* im Epilog. Es mag sinnvoll erscheinen, Pedalgebräuche aus **RR** zu übernehmen. Dagegen spricht jedoch nicht nur, dass Ravel kein erstklassiger Pianist war (wie seine Darbietung besonders der Valse I bezeugt), sondern auch, dass seine Einspielung von 1913 seine erste Begegnung mit dem Medium darstellte und nach allgemeiner Erfahrung der Pedalgebrauch zu jenen Aspekten gehört, die in Momenten nervlicher Anspannung zuallererst ins Wanken geraten. Die Bezeichnungen in **GarCP** stimmen nur teilweise mit dem Gebrauch in **RR** überein. Da sich in **CE** keine zusätzlichen Pedalangaben finden, obwohl Ravel jederzeit die Möglichkeit gehabt hätte, sie hier einzutragen, scheint es die beste Lösung, die Pedalisierung den Ausführenden zu überlassen. Hiervon ausgenommen sind jene Stellen, zu denen Perlemuter oder Faure spezielle Hinweise überliefern oder deren Pedalisierung in **RR** interessant und nicht durch technische Schwächen Ravels beeinträchtigt ist; in diesen Fällen wird das Nähere im Kritischen Bericht mitgeteilt.

### Verzeichnis der Quellensiglen

**AM**: Autograph auf Mikrofilm

**E**: Erstausgabe, bei Durand erschienen und am 28. Dezember 1911 bei der BNF hinterlegt (D&F. 8247)

**CE**: Ravels korrigiertes Exemplar der Erstausgabe

**CasCE**: Druckexemplar mit Zusätzen und Korrekturen von Casadesus

**GarCP**: Gedrucktes Korrekturexemplar mit Zusätzen und Korrekturen von Garban

**GarT**: Garbans Bearbeitung für Klavier zu vier Händen, 1918 bei Durand erschienen (D&F. 9549)

**PerCE**: Perlemuters Druckexemplar mit Zusätzen und Korrekturen von Ravel

**RO**: Ravels Bearbeitung für Orchester, 1912 bei Durand erschienen (D&F. 8476)

**RR**: Ravels Einspielung auf Klavierrolle

**CasR**: Einspielung von Casadesus

**FévR**: Einspielung von Février

**PerRI** und **PerRII**: Einspielungen von Perlemuter (die Bezeichnung **PerR** ohne Nummer bedeutet, dass die zwei Aufnahmen Perlemuters in Bezug auf den fraglichen Punkt übereinstimmen)

**PerS**: Erinnerungen von Perlemuter in *Ravel d'après Ravel*, im Gespräch mit Hélène Jourdan-Morhange

**FauS**: Erinnerungen von Faure in *Mon maître Maurice Ravel*

*Roger Nichols*
2007
Übersetzung: Arne Muus

---

[1] „Esquisse autobiographique", *La Revue Musicale* (Dez. 1938), 21

[2] Louis Aubert zu Manuel Rosenthal, der dem Herausgeber die Äußerung im Gespräch überlieferte.

[3] Vgl. Anmerkung 1, ebd.

[4] R. Howat: *The Piano music of Debussy, Ravel, Fauré and Chabrier. Explorations and illuminations*, Yale 2008, Kap. 17 (Ich danke dem Autoren, der es mir gestattete, das Typoskript des Buches zu sehen.)

[5] **PerS** 44/46

[6] *Les rencontres de M. de Bréot*, Paris 1904, 272f.

[7] Vgl. Anmerkung 1, ebd.

[8] Roland-Manuel, zit. n. **FauS** 37

[9] Mit herzlichem Dank an die Maison Durand, die mir Einblick in diese Zahlen gewährte.

[10] **PerS** 42/43

[11] **FauS** 20

[12] Nähere Angaben vgl. Deborah Mawer: *The Ballets of Maurice Ravel*, Aldershot 2006, 125-148.

[13] Enthalten auf einem Mikrofilm in der BNF, Vm. micr. 860.

# Valses nobles et sentimentales
## Adélaïde
«...le plaisir délicieux et toujours nouveau d'une occupation inutile.»
(Henri de Régnier)

Maurice Ravel
(1875–1937)

## I

Edition Peters No. 71000

© Copyright 2008 by Hinrichsen Editon, Peters Edition Ltd, London

## II

**Assez lent** – avec une expression intense ♩ = 104

## III

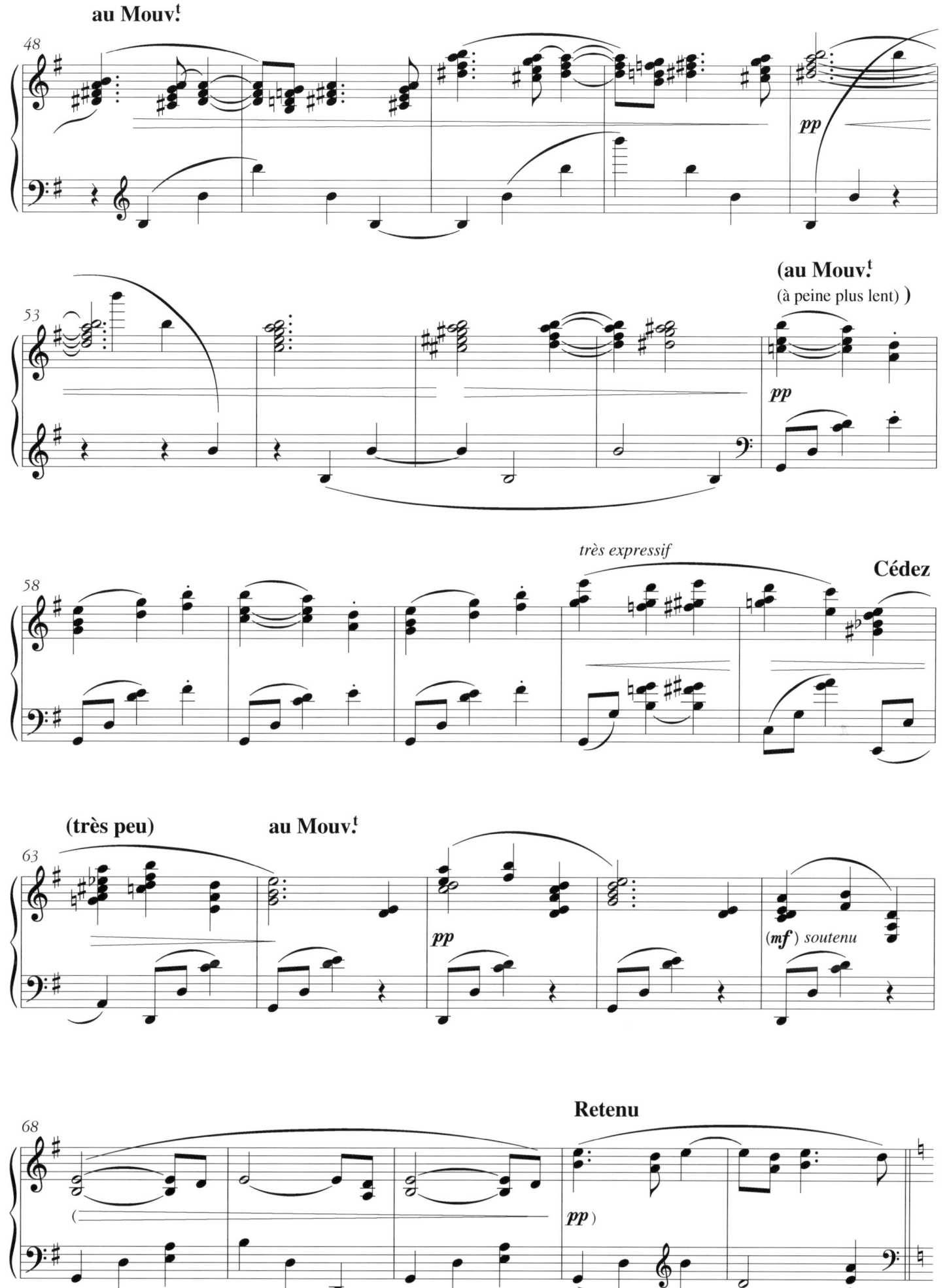

# IV

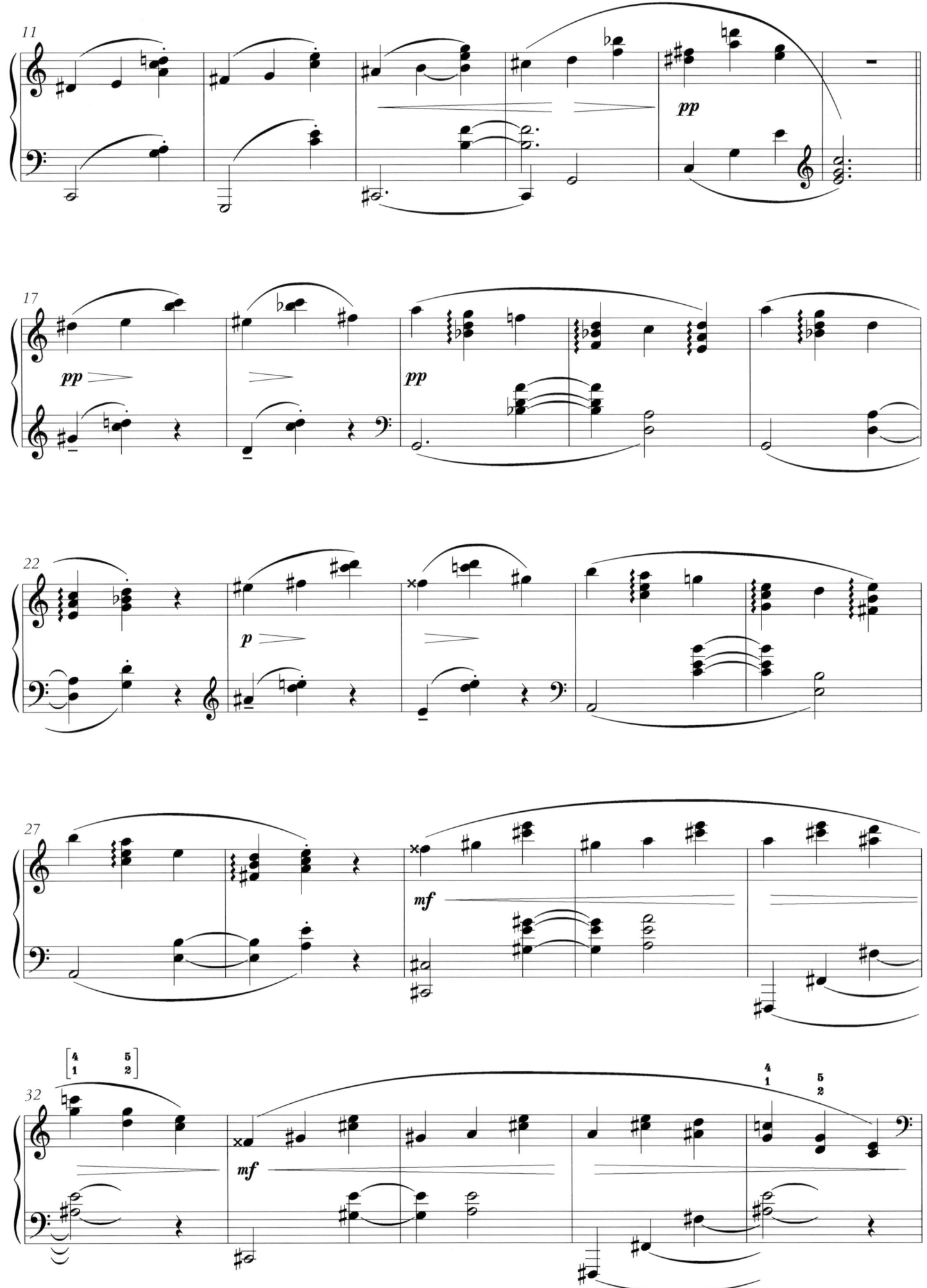

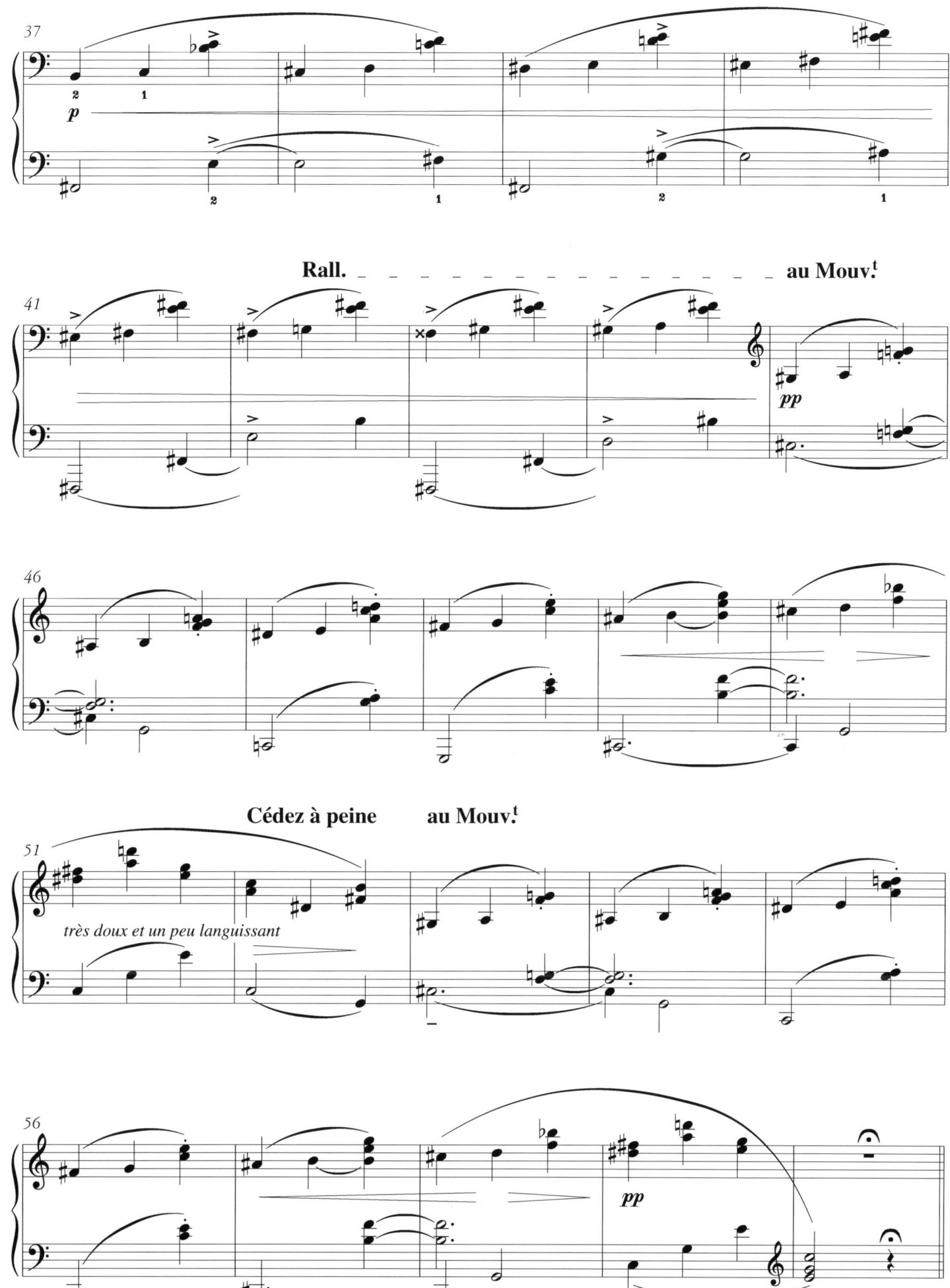

# VIII

★ see Critical Commentary

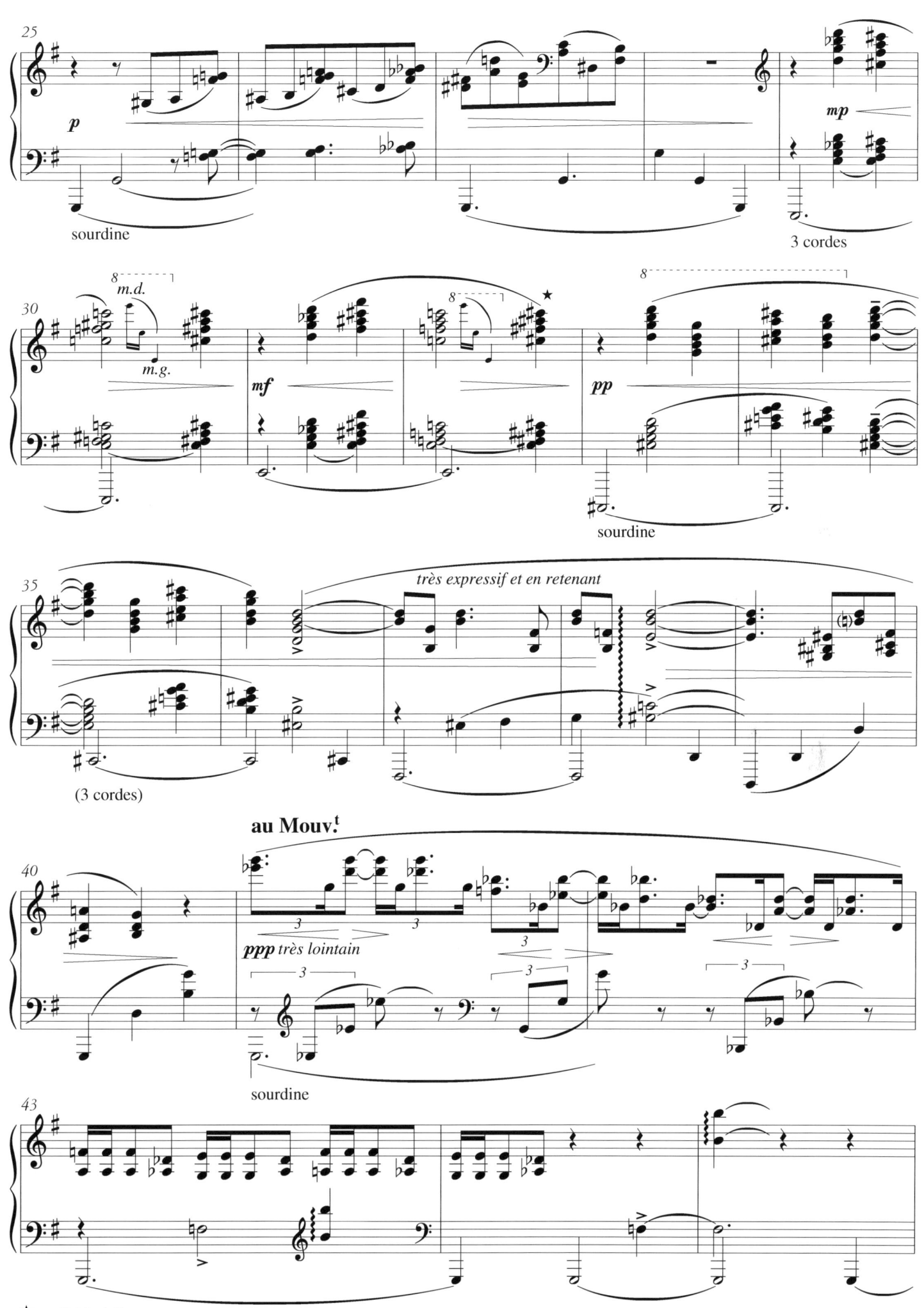

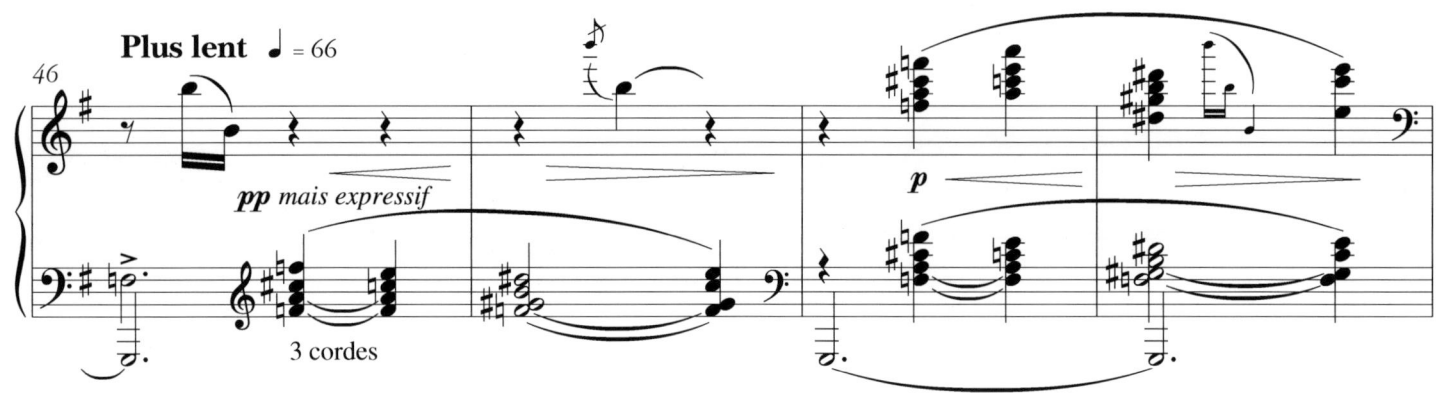

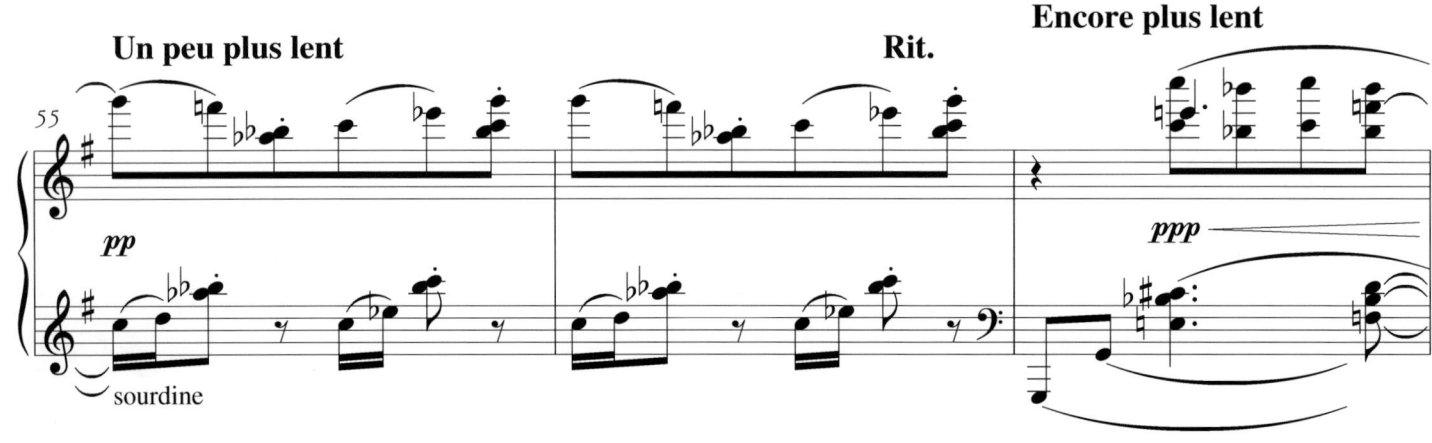

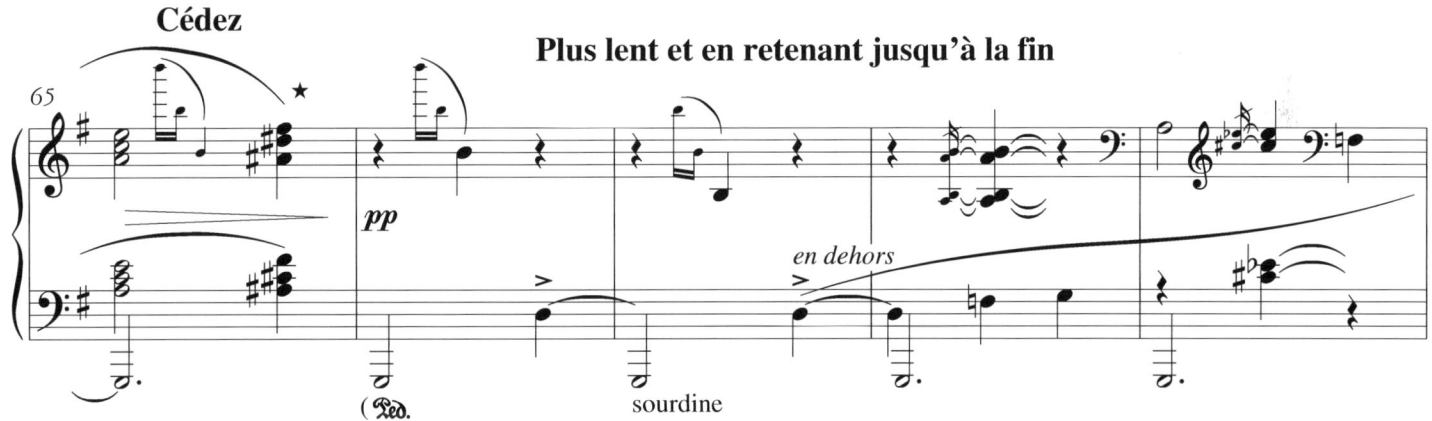
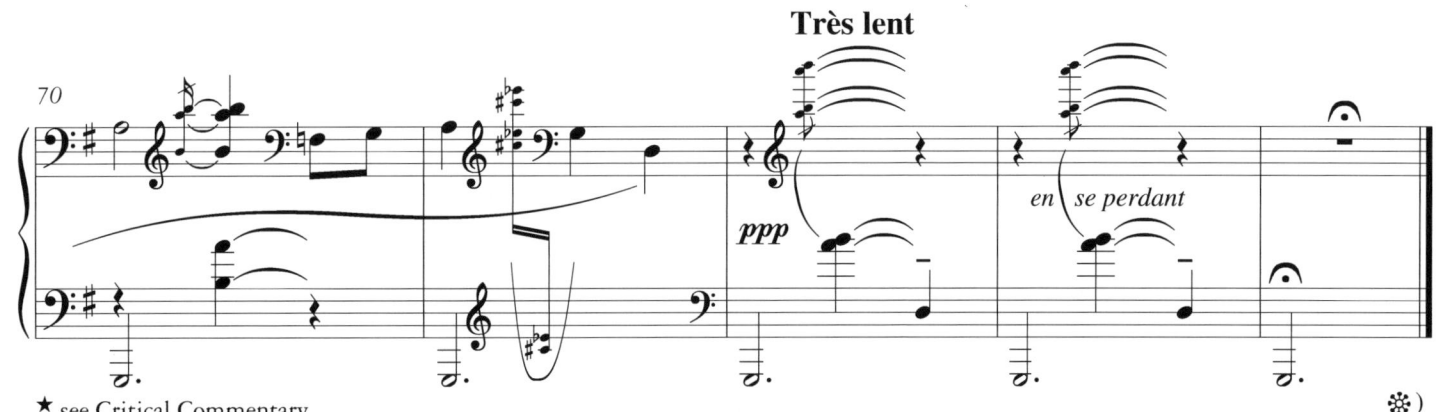

★ see Critical Commentary

# CRITICAL COMMENTARY

**AM** contains no metronome markings. All metronome markings taken from **E**

## I

Bars 1–4. According to Perlemuter, Ravel insisted that here and in parallel passages sustaining pedal should be depressed on quaver 1 and released on quaver 4 (information from Roy Howat). But **PerR** indicates rather pedal release on beat 3

Bars 15–18, 75–78. **RR** pedals from bar 15, beat 1 to bar 17, beat 1; then from bar 17, beat 2 to bar 18, beat 3; similarly in bars 75–78. **CasR**: bars 17–18, 77–78 without pedal. **FévR**: pedalling irregular. **PerR**: pedal on individual crotchets

Bars 33, 35. **PerS** 43/45: "Here, he [Ravel] wanted the emphasis on the second beat in the left hand to be well marked." ("Ici, il voulait l'appui bien marqué du second temps de la main gauche.")

Bars 45–60. **CasR** uses barely any sustaining pedal. **FévR** uses light pedal, increasing through bars 57–60 to support crescendo. **PerR** uses pedal to link individual crotchets

Bars 67–70. **PerS** 43/45: "Here, the singing left hand accentuates its binary rhythm. Ravel was very keen on this, which allows the pianist to bring it out." ("Ici, la main gauche chantante accentue son rythme binaire. Ravel y tenait beaucoup et cela permet de la mettre en dehors.")

Bars 73–77. Fingering on **AM**

## II

Bars 1–2. **AM**: crescendo hairpin from bar 1, beat 1 to bar 2, beat 2, then diminuendo (as in bars 3–4)

Bars 9–14. **GarCP**: sustaining pedal marked through single bars in bars 9,10, then 'simile'; observed, more or less, in **RR**. Also by **CasR**, **FévR**, **PerR**

Bars 15–16. **GarCP**: sustaining pedal marked through this pair of bars; observed in **RR**, **CasR**, **FévR**, **PerR**

Bar 19. **RO**: $p$

Bar 21. **RO**: $mf$

Bar 32. Pedal release indicated editorially. Not in any printed keyboard source

Bar 35. **RO**: $p$

Bar 36. **RO**: $f$. Crescendo hairpin shortened editorially to climax on beat 3

Bar 51. **RO**: $mf$

Bar 52. Diminuendo hairpin delayed editorially

Bar 53. **RO**: $mf$

Bars 63–64. **RO**, **RR**: diminuendo. Also **CasR**, **FévR**, **PerR**. **RO**: bar 63, beat 2, violins 2, added minim dyad $a\sharp/d'$, $a\sharp$ resolving up to $b$ in bar 64, with $d'$ tied over; followed in **GarT**

Bar 64. Pedal release indicated editorially. Not in any keyboard source.

## III

No metronome marking in any source. **CasR**: dotted minim=70; **FévR**: dotted minim=46; **PerRI**: dotted minim=65; **PerRII**: dotted minim=52. Although evidence from rolls as to absolute tempi is in general unreliable, **RR** would seem to lie towards faster end of this range

Bars 1–4. **AM**: here and in parallel passages, phrasing over all three RH crotchets. **PerS** 44/46: "The difficulty in this Valse is to isolate the third beat enough, which produces a hesitation before playing the first beat [of the next bar]." ("La difficulté de cette Valse est de bien isoler le troisième temps, cela donne une hésitation avant d'aborder le premier temps.")

Bars 1–4, 7–12, 14–16. **RR** meticulously observes LH crotchet rest, as well as syncopated phrasing in bars 5–6, 13–14

Bars 5–6. **RO**: crescendo and diminuendo

Bars 13–14. **RO**: crescendo and diminuendo

Bar 17. **RO**: $p$

Bars 17–23. **RR**: this passage more heavily pedalled. Also **CasR**, **FévR**, **PerR**. **PerS** 45/47: "After the double bar, the second episode must be played in a very singing style and Ravel insisted on the brief diminuendo that introduces the repetition of the phrase." ("Après la double barre, le second épisode doit être joué très chantant et Ravel tenait essentiellement au court diminuendo qui amène la répétition de la phrase.") 'Diminuendo' must refer to hairpin in bar 20. Re punctuation between bars 20 and 21, "Ravel said to me: 'like a curtsey'. The echo of this phrase is as if cut off. Ravel was so insistent on all this punctuation." ("Ravel m'avait dit: 'comme une révérence'. L'écho de cette phrase est comme brisé. Ravel insistait tellement sur toute cette ponctuation!") "Comme une révérence" in margin on **PerCE** in Perlemuter's hand

Bars 25–31. **RR** brings out syncopations. Also **CasR**, **FévR**, **PerR**

Bars 45, 47–48. Slurs added by analogy with surrounding bars

Bar 50. **AM**, **E**: RH, tie between $d''$s omitted. Inserted by Ravel on **CE**

Bar 57. **RO**: 'au Mouvt. (à peine plus lent)'. **RR** observes no change of tempo

Bars 57–60. **AM**: original phrasing throughout each bar corrected to present phrasing

Bars 62–63. **RO**: adds 'très peu' to 'Cédez'

Bar 67. **RO**: $mf$. No change of dynamics in **RR**

Bars 68–71. **RO**: diminuendo to ***pp***. **RR** makes crescendo to bar 69, beat 1, then diminuendo

## IV

**RO** has metronome marking crotchet=80, which must be in error

Bars 1–2. **PerS** 46/48: "As always, Ravel wanted the hairpin well emphasised, but without slowing down." ("Comme toujours, Ravel voulait le soufflet très marqué, mais sans s'attarder.")

Bars 2, 4. **AM**: diminuendo extended through whole of each bar

Bars 4, 7. 8. Fingering on **CE**

Bars 15–16. **AM**: RH phrasing originally to bar 15, beat 1, then separate phrase to bar 16, beat 1. Corrected on **AM**

Bar 26. **AM, E, GarCP, GarT**: RH, quaver 6, *d*𝄪″; **CE**:corrected by Ravel to *c*𝄪″, and thus in **RR**; **RO**: *d*♮″

Bar 29. As bar 26, except **AM** has *c*♯″

Bars 31–34. **PerCE, GarT**: again Perlemuter's claim (**PerS** 46/49) that Ravel added to LH a phrase from **RO** (octave cellos divisi, horns 1 and 4) in his own hand is hard to substantiate from **PerCE**. But since this MS addition is supported by **GarT**, it has been included in basic text. Dynamics have been changed to conform with **RO, GarT**. Since this extra line is not in **RR**, it must be assumed that Ravel realised possibility of inclusion only after 1913. In **PerR**; not in **CasR, FévR**

Bar 46. RH, staccato dot omitted from first time bar in some later editions. **PerS** 46/49: "Finally, I must underline the fact that Ravel was adamant about having the repeat as marked." ("Et pour finir, soulignons que Ravel tenait absolument à la reprise marquée.")

## V

**AM**: 'Presque' omitted

Bars 5–7, 29–31. **RO**: on inner *b*♯–*c*♯ octaves (oboe 1 + horn 3; then +horns 1, 2), *b*♯s stressed; observed in **RR**. Also in **CasR, PerR**

Bar 15. **AM, RR**: RH, quaver 2, *d*♯″; **GarCP**: *d*♯″ corrected to *f*♮″; **E, CE, GarT**: *f*♮″; **RO** (oboe 1): *f*♯″, possibly in error, since sharp is in key signature. **CasR, FévR, PerR**: *f*♮″

Bar 17. **AM**: ***ppp***

Bar 32. **RR**: sustaining pedal through this final bar. Also **CasR, PerR** (though with half-pedalling). Low E through bar in **GarT, RO** (bassoon 2)

## VI

**AM**: instead of metronome marking, there is autograph indication of '?=♪ du mouvt précédent'. Unfortunately, on microfilm value of ? is impossible to determine, though it looks rather like a semiquaver; this, however, would make no sense here. Metronome markings on **E**, printed here, might suggest 'dotted crotchet=♪ du mouvt précédent', but autograph marking cannot be interpreted thus; in any case, dotted crotchet is not a viable unit in Valse VI. **RR** is of no assistance in trying to establish metrical relationship

**RO**: time signatures alternate irregularly between 3/2 and 6/4. Those bars (1, 2, 5, 6 etc) where beat 3 is tied over bar are in 3/2, remainder in 6/4. This suggests Ravel was dissatisfied with pianists' observance of the triple/duple dichotomy, as supported by remarks in **PerS** 50/51–52, and by **CasR, PerR**.

Bars 36, 37. RH, fingering on **AM**

Bars 37–40. LH, fingering on **CE**

Bar 45. **AM, GarCP**: RH, beat 3, additional *c*♯′, deleted in **GarCP**

Bar 53. **AM, GarCP**: 'au Mouvt.' omitted; added in **GarCP**

Bar 55. **AM, GarCP, E**: RH, beat 3, chord contains *a*′, as in bar 3. In **PerCE**, this *a*′ is already beginning to fade, and in still later editions is reduced to a tiny stump

## VII

No metronome marking in any source. For Tempo 1o (bar 17), recorded tempi are: **CasR**: dotted minim=72; **FévR**: dotted minim=60; **PerRI**: dotted minim=74; **PerRII**: dotted minim=72

Bars 1–8. Dynamics from **RO**; at least suggested in **RR**. In **FévR, PerR**

Bars 6–7. Resonance ties added editorially to conform with bars 2–3

Bar 9. **RO**: 'Un peu retenu'

Bar 17. **AM, RO**: 'Modéré'; **GarCP**: deleted, replaced with 'Tempo 1o'

Bars 19–20. **FauS**: Ravel asked Fauré "to delay slightly the right hand chord in the second bar" ("de faire légèrement attendre l'accord de la deuxième mesure à la main droite")

Bar 22. RH, later editions have added erroneous augmentation dots to minim

Bars 24–28. **PerS** 52/54: "Ravel wanted this phrase to go beyond being expressive, as it's marked, and to be, as he said, 'expansive'." ("Ravel demandait cette phrase, plus qu'expressive, comme elle est marquée, mais comme il la dit: 'expansive'.")

Bars 28, 120. **AM, GarT, E, CE, RR, CasR, FévR, PerR**: RH, beat 1, upper note e'; **RO, GarT**: *f*♯′. On this evidence, reading of e' seems preferable, though *f*♯′ has its charms

Bars 39, 131. **RR** accelerates sharply here both times, certainly not out of desire to make life easy. Not followed by **CasR, FévR, PerR**

Bars 55, 147. **FauS**: "Ravel wanted here again a great flight of Romanticism produced on the chord on the second beat . . ." ("Ravel voulait encore ici une grande envolée romantique par l'accent donné sur l'accord du 2e temps . . .")

Bars 59, 151. **AM**: no pause

Bar 64. **AM**: beat 2, both hands marked with -

Bar 66. **RR, FévR** make absolutely no pause before 'Un peu plus animé' section. **CasR, PerRII** make short pause, **PerRI** slightly longer one. **PerS** 52/55: "Although the marking here is 'très doux', he [Ravel] asked me to bring the tune out very distinctly." ("Quoique marqué 'très doux', il m'avait demandé ici le chant très en dehors.") **FauS** 42: Ravel described the sound of this section as of "a musical box gone haywire"("une boîte à musique détraquée")

Bar 70. RH, fingering on **AM**

Bars 70, 74. RH, augmentation dots to minims added editorially

Bars 77–78. RH, fingering on **AM**

Bar 93. RH, augmentation dot added editorially

Bar 99. **AM**: RH, beat 3, $d'$ and $b\flat$ quavers reversed, as in bar 101

Bars 106–111. RH, phrasing added as in **GarT** and as suggested by bars 17–19

Bars 111, 114. LH, beat 3, tenuto markings added as in bars 19 and 22, and as in **GarT**

Bar 156. **AM**: beat 2, both hands marked with $>$; altered editorially to $-$, to conform with bar 64

## VIII

Bar 1. **AM**: 'et en dehors' omitted. Precautionary '3 cordes' added editorially, following **CasCE**, **PerCE**, necessary before 'sourdine' in bar 5

Bar 9, etc. **PerS** 54/57: 'The grace notes, the ornaments, must not be casual, even though they're played softly, and must come very precisely on the beat.' ('Les petites notes, les ornements ne doivent pas être flous, même dans la douceur, et doivent tomber très exactement sur le temps.')

Bar 12. **AM, GarCP, E, CE, GarT, CasR, FévR, PerR**: beat 3, chord as printed here. **RO**: chord $a/c\sharp/d\sharp/f\sharp$. **RR**: $a/b/d\sharp/f\sharp$. Ravel's uncharacteristic indecision possibly caused by repeat of $a\sharp/b\sharp$ as $a\sharp/c\natural$ in bar 13, where change of chord arguably more elegant

Bars 27–28. **RR, PerR** hold sustaining pedal through these two bars, possibly adding to impact of low E' in bar 29

Bar 29. **AM**: '3 cordes' omitted in error

Bars 30, 32. **AM, GarCP, E, CE, RO, RR**: on beat 3 of each bar, the As are natural, then sharp. Worth mentioning, as **FévR, PerRII** play A$\sharp$s in both places; **CasR, PerRI**: as printed. **GarCP**: beat 3, $e$ deleted in both bars; but restored in **E, CE**

Bars 33–41. Since both terminal bars are marked 'sourdine', a '3 cordes' has to be inserted somewhere in this passage. **CasCE** puts it at bar 35, as suggested here

Bars 41–74. **GarT**, following **RO**, gives continuous low $G'$ or $G$ or both until the end of the piece

Bar 45. **RR**: all sound released at end of beat 2, $G'$ retaken with sustaining pedal

Bar 46–47. **AM**: 'Plus lent' omitted. **AM, RO**: crescendo to bar 47, beat 1

Bars 50–54. **RR, PerRI**: increase of speed from bar 50, beat 1 to 'Cédez'

Bars 55–59. Since both terminal bars are marked 'sourdine', a '3 cordes has to be inserted somewhere in this passage. Bar 58, beat 2 suggested editorially, where woodwind enter in **RO**

Bar 57. **AM**: 'Encore un peu plus lent'

Bar 58. LH, quaver 6, editorial cautionary natural before $a'$

Bar 62. **AM**: '1er Mouvt…' instead of 'même Mouvt…'

Bar 65. **AM, GarCP, E, CE, GarT, CasR, FévR, PerR**: beat 3, chords as printed; **RO, RR**: B major triads

Bars 66, 67. Perlemuter recommended taking crotchets $b'$ and $b$ with LH (information from Roy Howat).

Bars 66, 67, 72, 73. **GarCP**: LH, $d$s indicated 'm.d.' As this not taken over on to **E**, possibly noted by Garban merely for his own convenience; but swing of RH across body may help achieve marked accentuation on these four notes. Perlemuter also recommended this

Bars 66–74. **RR**: LH, $G'$ held through these nine bars with sustaining pedal

Total timings: **CasR**: 12'48"; **FévR**: 15'40"; **PerR**: 14'02", remarkably, for both recordings